# CARLOS JIMENEZ *Buildings*

# CARLOS JIMENEZ *Buildings*

PHOTOGRAPHS BY PAUL HESTER

ARCHITECTURE AT RICE 36

RICE UNIVERSITY SCHOOL OF ARCHITECTURE, HOUSTON

PRINCETON ARCHITECTURAL PRESS, NEW YORK

1996

Published by the Rice School of Architecture; Lars Lerup, Dean
and Princeton Architectural Press; Kevin C. Lippert, Publisher


*Published on the occasion of the dedication of the*
*Spencer Studio Art Building, Williams College, April 12-13, 1996*


Design: Dung Ngo and Carlos Jiménez
Executive editor: Dung Ngo
Special thanks: Linda Shearer, Richard Newlin,
Stephen Fox, Gina Cariño, Chad Johnson, Mark Lamster.
Printed & bound in Hong Kong


© Rice School of Architecture                    *and*
Architecture at Rice Publications            Princeton Architectural Press
6100 South Main                              37 East Seventh Street
Houston, Texas 77005-1892                    New York, New York 10003
713 527-4864                                 212 995-9620

Library of Congress Cataloguing-in-Publication
Jiménez, Carlos, 1959-
Carlos Jiménez : buildings / photographs by Paul Hester.
p.    cm -- (Architecture at Rice : 36)
Includes bibliographical references.
ISBN: 1-885232-05-5 (alk. paper)
1. Jimenez, Carlos, 1959-    --Themes, motives.   2. Architecture,
Postmodern--United States.   I. Hester, Paul.   II. Title.   III. Series:
Architecture at Rice ; no. 36.
NA1.A785  no. 36
[NA 737. J53]
720 s--dc20                          96-20166
[720' .92]                           CIP

# CONTENTS

# Introduction
*Rafael Moneo*

Cultured architecture and public architecture have become practically synonymous, since public architecture -- that used by institutions -- has always served as a framework for formal invention. Public architecture is therefore a testing ground where architects can carry out the linguistic inquiries implicit in the continuous evolution towards which the inevitable passage of time happily pushes them. In history we witness the forging of manners and elements which, following criteria that are not always too clear, come to form part of the architecture that served the interests of the domestic and the private and ends up being called anonymous, popular or vernacular, after having shown those concerned with the study of these manners and elements how many of what we now consider their characteristic features are but versions of others -- sometimes remote in time and space -- on which the common sense of the straightforward builder was grafted. Though hard to believe, the winds of architecture have led us from the public to the private, from institutional to domestic architecture, from the temple to the house.

May the foregoing reflection serve to begin another on the works by Carlos Jiménez presented in this book. All could be classified as public buildings. Work places such as his own architectural design studio or a printer's; buildings open to the public such as the "Drive-in Library", or the bank in Columbus, Indiana; art spaces like the Lynn Goode Gallery; and finally, institutional buildings serving educational and administrative functions at the same time, such as the Art League of Houston, and those built for the Museum of Fine Arts, Houston or the Spencer Studio Art Building at Williams College. Though located miles apart and address-ing very different briefs, they have something in common. What characterizes and let us see them as a compact and consistent whole? Simply, this handful of buildings represents a pleasing and unexpected turnabout by closing the circle that led from public to private, since these works of Carlos Jiménez show us how domestic architecture can serve as a stimulus and become a basis for public architecture. It could not have happened any other way. He spent years involved in building one-family houses and the experience accumulated through private commissions is now transferred to the public sphere without undue difficulty.

Carlos Jiménez does not alter his way of tackling architecture, and thus we find before us a series of public works in which attention to the specific prevails - whether the program, the place or the materials. The attention given to a beautiful tree, the difficulties implicit in a slope, the desire to enjoy a view of the landscape from one's work place, the use of color as a catalyst of spaces, the excitement one always feels with crossing the threshold of a house, the pleasure of shifting from one material to another, which is like what the painter experiences as he handles the colors of his palette, .... -- all this lies at the base of an architecture in which clarity and complexity are not contradictory. And such has always been the architecture of Carlos Jiménez. His houses have exemplarily proved that it is possible to cater to the individual, through unique spaces and programs, while respecting the larger community, manifest in the exquisite care with which these address the exigencies of their particular context.

But the innovative thing about these works is the fact that criteria used in domestic and private architectures are efficiently applied to institutional and public buildings. The result is public architecture that does not intimidate, that does not try to overwhelm or impress through sheer size or scale. Public architecture that takes pride in being rational instead of indulging in rhetorical elements aimed at wielding artificial authority;

it seeks what is natural, avoiding all exaggeration and waste. This is a new face -- and the only possible face -- of public architecture, the architecture of institutions.

Such an attitude implies a great deal of social maturity, but though of crucial importance, this is not the thing to dwell on at present. What most impresses me about Carlos Jiménez is his capacity to perceive the world from the viewpoint of architecture, whatever the situation, and always with a Franciscan generosity reflecting the deep-seated love and compassion that a creation deserves. To Carlos Jiménez, all architectures are equally worthy of attention and all must be treated with the same respect. Institutions and individuals, public and private, are treated in the same way. There is no difference between one and the other. The architectural experience is one and the same and he makes no distinction between the space of the house and that of the temple. The same architecture that exalts the intimate and private in the domestic space can be applied to a library or a bank. Square-shaped windows looking onto pleasant landscapes, handsome staircases dominating the space, light suspended canopies protecting the entrances, the artful firmament of the roofs... We are familiar with these elements, which Carlos Jiménez previously used in his houses. As we said at the beginning of these notes, the tendency of architecture to move from the public to the private has happily changed its course in the works presented here. The architecture of Carlos Jiménez confirms that the quest for plenitude does not rule out audacity.

March 1996                                        *Translated by Gina Cariño*

# The Sky in the House

*Stephen Fox*

Carlos Jiménez's buildings compel you with their directness and simplicity.
They delight with playful seriousness. Their bold colors imply a flush of
enthusiasm that has momentarily broken through the veneer of shyness.
Jiménez animates architecture by tapping into the energies latent in line
and plane. He subordinates formal distractions in order to invest line and
plane with visual resonance, acoustic resonance, and ultimately to stir more
subjective layers of experience, such as memory and emotion. These
operations are subtle rather than theatrical. It is as though experience is
always being filtered through the refining medium of Jiménez's sensibility,
to distill it and re-present it in spatial equivalents of poetic condensation.
This is apparent in the way his architecture responds to nature, which it
frames, filters, and condenses, but almost always from a distance. This
distance interposes a kind of spatial insulation, from which Jiménez's
buildings derive their sense of composure and tranquillity, however bold
their coloration, or out-of-control their surroundings.

The Blue Studio condenses a sense of what Carlos Jiménez's architecture is
about. The figural profile of the studio's frontal plane, the saturated blue
of its stucco walls, and the calculated arrangement of its windows, which
sustain the planarity of the façade with their implication of volumetric
depth, are immediately evident. As you approach the Blue Studio, walking
past what was originally the Red House, you see through the upper window
what looks like an optical illusion: a framed vista of the sky, almost the
same color as the stucco wall plane. You have to look twice to realize that
you are seeing the sky--through a high window on the studio's rear wall.
The realization is exhilirating. It makes you feel like you just discovered a
secret view of the world no one had ever seen before. Above the front door
is a thin metal canopy whose tense deflection insinuates danger. Is it about
to collapse? Standing nervously beneath it, you hear your knocking
reverberate inside. Between the closed blinds of the window next to the

door, a slit is opened. The door is then unlocked with a snap of solidity and, as it swings open, you have an uncanny sense that you are walking into the opening sequence of a movie. There is something enigmatic and portentous about the way a white diagonal wall plane slices the space you enter. If it is early evening, vertical panels of glass block along the side wall burn with the suffused intensity of the setting sun. From somewhere in the depths of the interior, a Mexican diva wails in desolation. If this were the beginning of a movie, would it be a *film noir*?

The subtlety, complexity, and sly humor of Jiménez's buildings (he had to insert a metal prop beneath the canopy because callers were so apprehensive) might strike observers as out of place in the raucousness of Houston. Jiménez's architecture exhibits few obvious connections to any cultural imagery that might be identified as Houstonian or Texan. What his buildings posit is the transposition of a Latin American architectural sensibility to Houston, a tendency first noted by Joel Warren Barna in the buildings that the Mexican architect Ricardo Legorreta has produced in Texas. Less obtrusively than Legorreta, Jiménez purposefully and consistently plugs leaky urban space in Houston. He re-urbanizes the shredded fabric of Houston's inner-city precincts by infusing his buildings with a typological discipline that is Hispanic in origin.

If one looks at the Hispanic architects who have achieved prominence in the U.S. since the 1970s, it is evident that their work, like Jiménez's, resists stylistic classification as Hispanic. Legorreta, the Argentine émigrés (César Pelli, Emilio Ambasz, Diana Agrest and Mario Gandelsonas, and Rodolfo Machado and Jorge Silvetti), the Cuban Andrés Duany, and the Peruvian Bernardo Fort-Brescia espouse positions that are diverse, even antagonistic. To the extent that one can discern a common denominator among them, it is a predilection for architecture as urbanism. One should not have to argue that this is a culturally exclusive preoccupation to note that it figures strongly in the work of almost all of these architects. One of the most incisive examinations of the phenomenon of architecture as urbanism in U.S. architectural publication has been the typological analysis of towns and buildings in southern and western Puerto Rico by Jorge Rigau. Rigau demonstrates how traditional *criollo* building types held Puerto Rican cities together, even while absorbing external architectural influences, well into the 20th century. In Texas, this tendency is visible in the cities of the Texas-Mexican border. The historic Casa Leyendecker in Laredo, which Jiménez rehabilitated as an office for the lawyer Ricardo De

Anda, exemplifies the L-plan, Creole, patio house, which as the historian and critic Richard Ingersoll has observed, is the archetype of so many of Jiménez's buildings. While a student in the late 1970s and early 1980s, Jiménez discovered in the writings and architecture of Aldo Rossi convictions and a sensibility that strongly affected him. Jiménez's architecture is grounded in the discipline of type, and it has enabled him to reclaim, through Rossi's agency, a *criollo* spatial legacy with which to confront the anarchic spatiality of modern Texas.

When he presents his work in lectures, Jiménez frequently illustrates rural and vernacular buildings from Costa Rica, where he was born and grew up. Their figured profiles, intense colors, and occasionally haunting spaces suggest sensations that Jiménez has sought to parallel in his own buildings. Yet however poignantly Jiménez speaks of these images, he does not seem motivated to reproduce the nostalgia they evoke in him. Jiménez's work may seem conservative because of its typological discipline. But he has not attempted to codify the retrospective potential of type or prescribe neo-conservative interpretations of his work.

In the manner of vernacular buildings, Jiménez's urbanism is matter-of-fact, even opportunistic. This can be seen in the way that he makes space in Houston. At the Houston Fine Art Press Building, he used a high, blank wall to surround the property and insert spatial definition into the Gulfton corridor, an amorphous in-between zone that became Houston's Central American refugee neighborhood in the 1980s. From outside, the wall invisible-izes. It causes the Fine Art Press Building to disappear amid the parallel rows of rental warehouses that adjoin it. From inside, the wall shapes a spatial foreground for the building, which is no less effective for being a parking lot. The walled enclosure--distilling, refining, visually editing--emphasizes the presence of the sky in order to produce a spatial sensation of undistracting, unobsessive intensity, invoking the outdoor spaces of the Mexican architect Luis Barragán. The Fine Art Press Building's gray-painted steel street gate, composed of slender, closely spaced vertical bars, is an explicit homage to the gates that Barragán used at the Jardines del Pedegral.

Jiménez's buildings invoke another of his heroes, the Spanish film director Luis Buñuel. A prime example occurs at the Fine Art Press Building. Halfway between the building's strongly colored, simply gabled front elevation and its back end, he shifted section. Jiménez widened the floor plate of the rear half of the building, so that it spans from side lot line to side lot line, and inserted a high, north-facing clerestory to compensate for the resulting loss of side light. He accomplished this by transforming the building's gabled section into an arc and shed with such deftness that, unless one saw the building being framed, the ingenuity of this geometric operation is not immediately apparent. Just as the narratives of Buñuel's films of the 1960s slid without warning from the ordinary into the outrageous, then back to the ordinary, so Jiménez delights in solving practical problems with sly spatial transformations.

Buñuel and Barragán--the radical atheist satirist and the Catholic gentleman-aesthete--correspond to different facets of Jiménez's sensibility, his propensities for being both trickster and contemplative. In his buildings, one sees these inclinations sublimated in line and plane. Planarity is as intrinsic to Jiménez's architecture as typological grounding. To use a movie-making term, it "establishes" the essential calmness of his architecture. In his buildings, the plane is repeatedly energized by the activated diagonal line. Although Jiménez used diagonals and arcs planimetrically in his earliest work (such as the Artist's Studio), he made an exception when he designed the Red House (now painted blue and part of his "empire," as Simone Swan calls his studio compound). There, the diagonal appears only in section. It slices space, rather than reorienting it axially. It relieves the static intensity of the plane. Jiménez experimented with the activating diagonal line when he juxtaposed the main stair of the Lynn Goode Gallery to the principal gallery space, a double volume containing one high-set window. He spatialized the diagonal, transforming it from a bounding line into a spiraling volume, which ascends toward the inclined plane of the ceiling. The stair is not theatrical; it is not supposed to distract attention from the art on display. Instead, it induces a sense of imaginary movement (in addition to the more pedestrian sort, of course), a cerebral ascent that relieves and refreshes. In Jiménez's architecture, the diagonal activates the section in order to liberate space.

Jiménez's stucco-surfaced buildings pose the problem of applied color. Following Latin American practice, he has routinely applied paint to stucco walls as a protective coating. Following Latin American practice, Jiménez has routinely specified brightly colored paint. Architects tend to distrust applied color--and question its use--because it is pretty and fun; it embarrasses their pretensions to seriousness, permanence, and dignity. It is also fugitive. The sun bleeds it; humidity streaks and stains it. The effusive application of color in architecture tends to be a vernacular rather than high style trait. Legorreta, the most coloristic of contemporary architects, cites folkloric examples as his inspiration. Barragán also applied color to his architecture, but with far greater asperity than Legorreta. Does color make Jiménez's buildings merely cute? Would they possess the same magnetism if chromatically neutral? An evasive answer to these questions is that color infuses the static plane with ecstatic intensity. It ambiguously charges, without inducing perceived movement or focusing an observer's attention. Applied color is what might be characterized as an "undecidable" attribute of Jiménez's architecture. Strong color causes his buildings to resonate with equivocation. Therefore, one experiences his use of applied color as penetrating rather than decorative, especially because exterior color tends to be twinned with the white, high-lit world of a Jiménez interior, where the tension induced by equivocation is released and absorbed in space.

The window in Jiménez's buildings also animates, but in a way that differs from the activating diagonal and applied color. It tends to project an implied spatial dimension into the plane that gives the plane weight and density. At the Lynn Goode Gallery, the frontality of the orange stucco façade derives its urbanistic authority from the intimation of depth produced by the shallow layering of planes behind the primary plane. Square-sectioned windows do not so much afford vistas into the interior as they imply the existence of staged depths, with the façade suspended in a tense balance between aspect and interior.

From inside, the window projects, relieves, and abstracts. Jiménez takes advantage of these attributes by framing prospects. The views of live oak trees from the second-story windows of the Lynn Goode Gallery are so captivating that they do sometimes compete with the art on display. Jiménez has spoken of what he considers the role of abstraction in architecture: to concentrate attention and awareness. From inside, his windows abstract elements of the surrounding landscape and intensify their presence, while framing out whatever might distract. Despite his love of natural light and his use of large glazed openings, Jiménez is careful never to confuse the window and the wall of glass. This is consistent with his compositional preferences. It also expresses the value he places on interiority. Jiménez is quite convivial. But only when work is done. He is very private and very focused. In his studio compound, he tends to keep window blinds drawn, not to darken the interiors but to diffuse the intense sunlight of Houston and screen the inside from prying eyes. Typically, it is the high "sky" windows in his buildings that are left unobstructed. Like the panels of glass block that he uses to liquefy natural light, they illuminate what one might call the imaginary space of Jiménez's interiors.

Among Jiménez's public buildings, one project stands out as an exception, the Drive-In Library. It is unprecedented in being bi-axially symmetrical and having a flat roof. It has no site, which means it would probably rise from a surface parking lot alongside a wide, arterial strip or a freeway frontage road. A hypothetical design produced for the exhibition *Project: Houston*, organized at DiverseWorks Artspace by Deborah V. Brauer, the Drive-In Library is totally polemical, in a way that even Jiménez's buildings for himself are not. It engages a discourse about Houston as the anti-city of incessant movement and uncertain culture. It was conceived as a typological hybrid: part drive-in bank, drive-in fast food restaurant, and gas station. The diagonal members that span from the entry columns to the edges of the thick roof lid evoke the image of a windmill, like those that don Quixote confronted. Perhaps this should be interpreted as a cautionary warning of the futility of trying to reform the suburban landscape of Houston and similar cities through architecture alone. It is also tempting to interpret the Drive-In Library project as an exploration of formal possibilities to which Jiménez was not yet prepared to commit in a building project. The fixated quality that derives from Jiménez's combination of symmetry, big scale, and top heavy profile suggests that he was critically reappraising a generation of buildings constructed in Houston between the mid-1930s and early 1950s, which the architect Howard Barnstone once derisively categorized as "out of phase" modern. Although the Drive-In Library ostensibly represents a coming to terms with the landscape of suburban sprawl, its significance for Jiménez's subsequent buildings is that it signaled his willingness to look for architectural inspiration to what Robert Venturi and Denise Scott-Brown might describe as the "dumb" and "ordinary" modern vernacular buildings produced in Houston in the 1940s and '50s, seeing in these the means to recover the possibility of a modern urban architecture.

It is intriguing that Jiménez (like such Spanish architects as Martínez Lapeña & Torres and Guillermo Vázquez Consuegra, or his Mexican contemporary Alberto Kalach) should gravitate toward varieties of sub-modern or semi-modern architecture that, in part because they retained a strong urban bias, were considered antithetical to the modern architectural tendencies critically approved of in Texas since the 1930s. Texan traditions of modern architecture have tended to emphasize tectonics, materials, and (implicitly suburban) site relationships on the one hand. One the other, they have involved stylistic discipleship and the domestication of received imagery. In Houston, there has been a consistent preference for the latter alternative. This led to the production of a large body of significant modern architecture in the second half of the 20th century. But it is architecture that often seems to reference other places (and other personalities), not Houston. Efforts by such architects as John F. Staub, Houston's great eclectic architect, and the modernist Howard Barnstone, to produce urban architecture that was in some respect Houstonian were sporadic, although quite interesting. One example of this phenomenon is especially pertinent to Jiménez: the house-studio and garden that his friend and former teacher, John Zemanek, designed and built between 1957 and 1968. Zemanek adapted Japanese attitudes and sensibilities in his design of an affordable house in an existing neighborhood. He demonstrated the possibility of intensifying, particularizing--or in Houston terminology, "developing"--urban space in Houston to invest it with the sense of cultural depth and specificity that the city seems to lack. The Zemanek House is one of the stylistically discontinuous examples of a heterogeneous school of Houston architecture within which Jiménez's buildings might be situated. This is a "constructed" tradition, based not on type, style, or materials, but on architects' efforts to make a home out of Houston.

Where Jiménez does intersect local tradition is with the patronage network through which his commissions have come. The socio-cultural thread that binds his work together is art: its production, collection, and sale. Almost all of his public buildings (as well as many of his houses) share the art connection. This places his architecture in an elitist context. Not in the sense that it reinforces exclusionary or anti-democratic impulses, but in the sense that its audience consists of privileged individuals and institutional representatives who value personal vision, singular authorship, and custom production. In this respect, Jiménez is heir to a Houston tradition of modern architectural patronage stemming from the collectors Dominique Schlumberger and John de Menil, although he has never worked for Mrs. de Menil or any of the Menil institutions.

Menil architectural patronage has been important in Houston not only because of the buildings with which the Menils were directly involved, but because of its spill-over effect on other architects and their clients.  Mr. and Mrs. de Menil set a precedent for architectural anti-provincialism, to which institutional and entrepreneurial clients in Houston came to adhere. This was apparent as early as 1954 when the Museum of Fine Arts, at the instigation of the Houston architects Hugo V. Neuhaus, Jr., and Anderson Todd, retained Ludwig Mies van der Rohe to prepare a master plan for completion of the museum building.  Because of Menil patronage, modern architecture that was austere, unassertive, yet urbane--that could provide regular volumes, clear light, and generous proportions for the display of art--came to be coded in Houston as patrician and, within certain circles, preferred to other, more demonstrative modern tendencies.  Austerity entailed the rejection of formal eccentricity, which enhanced the appeal of Menil modernism in Houston by positioning it, ironically, as a conservative alternative.  Jiménez's professional involvement with the Menil circle has been peripheral: he was an occasional collaborator of Howard Barnstone, and he designed one of his largest houses for the widow of Hugo Neuhaus. The significance of the Menil dispensation for his career is that it produced a cultural climate (granted, one that is quite rarefied) in which a young immigrant who had limited professional experience before beginning independent practice, and is not a licensed architect, could secure the building commissions that Jiménez has.

An element of Menil sensibility related to Jiménez's architecture deserves mention.  This is a predilection for surrealism (the Menil Collection possesses major collections of the works of René Magritte and Max Ernst). Spatially, surrealism colored the precinct within which Renzo Piano's Menil Collection museum was built in the 1980s.  In 1974 Howard Barnstone painted all the bungalow houses surrounding the future museum site gray-green.  Chromatic uniformity had the curious property of emphasizing formal differences among individual houses, even as it superficially made them all alike.  Jiménez's buildings seem privy to this secret of how to achieve more by doing less.  The hypnotic image of the sky in the house visible at the Blue Studio could be a spatial transcription from Magritte.  It is also tempting to draw a parallel between the Rothko Chapel, which Mr. and Mrs. de Menil built to contain the paintings made for it by Mark Rothko, and Jiménez's objectives as an architect.  Rothko's paintings are obscure mirrors that reflect and absorb consciousness.  They work with the architecture of Barnstone and Eugene Aubry's chapel to spatialize a quiet so profound that it makes a place in which mortality can be contemplated. One gets something of this sense in Jiménez's buildings.  Over and above meeting their practical obligations, they provide space for the experience of time stilled, for introspection, and the possibility of renewal. Rothko's and Jiménez's affinity for the plane (like Magritte's and Jiménez's for the window) suggests a straining at the limits of art to communicate human experiences that can be intimated with more precision than they can be described or prescribed.

It is intriguing to examine Jiménez's architecture in terms of the work that Donald Judd installed and built at the Chinati Foundation outside Marfa, Texas, about which Jiménez has written. What Jiménez's buildings have in common with Judd's installations in Marfa is a fascination with shaping surfaces whose apparent formal simplicity is gradually revealed to be complex, varied, and unpredictable. The writer and critic Elizabeth McBride has noted how exposure to Judd's installations at the Chinati Foundation transforms one's awareness, so that certain architectural phenomena, the result of Judd's subtractive and abstracting process of building rehabilitation, engage the art and the viewer in profound yet uncoercive ways. In much the same way, Jiménez's buildings, rather than treating their occupants as involuntary witnesses to theatrical spectacles, sensitize them to the possibility of experiential discovery.

As a Central American and the recipient of a Catholic education, Jiménez was predisposed to benefit from the privileged space that the Menils opened up in Houston, a space in which their Catholic social activism and liberal theological inquiry made it seem reasonable to search works of art for their spiritual dimensions. In talking about his architecture, Jiménez uses terminology that harkens more to his upbringing than it does discourses current among vanguard U.S. architects. He invokes "purity," for instance, which to Anglo-American ears has a slightly sinister ring. Yet in his Central Administration and Glassell Junior School Building for the Museum of Fine Arts, Jiménez spatializes the experience of purity in the building's entrance vestibule. At night, when its free-standing, marble-clad elevator shaft, rimmed by the ascending diagonal of an open-riser, glass-railed stair, is back and top lit, the vestibule is glistering in its whiteness, as it is during the day when penetrated by the morning or late afternoon sun. This space could so easily be experienced as slick, pretentious, sterile, or vacuous. Instead, it is luminous, refreshing, purifying. Its intensity is cinematic: composed, yet accommodating real-time movement and action. Shortly after the building was opened, the Rice Design Alliance held a reception there. Three jazz musicians performed on the top level of the vestibule. They suffused Jiménez's tall, white space with the cool, plaintive music of a blues saxophone, keyboard, and guitar, which swelled as it spiraled downward to fill the pristine volume.

The sensation of being purified is not one commonly associated with Houston office buildings. The Administration and Junior School Building impresses the more one experiences and examines it because it is so inventive and yet, in the phrase of Allison and Peter Smithson, "without rhetoric." Jiménez dispensed with the office building type that tyrannizes the imaginations of Houston architects (and their clients): the floor plate of neutral space radiating in equal depth from a central vertical core and enveloped by curtain walls. He did this so he could shape the Administration and Junior School Building as a public building (in the sense that the Italian word *palazzo* connotes public building, even when it is used for an office building) and, at the same time, fundamentally re-shape the clerical workplace in Houston.

Jiménez purposefully deployed the building's long, thin block shape to reinforce the corridor space of Montrose Boulevard, architecturally backing up the Masterson oaks, planted along the sidewalk line of the site in the 1920s, and the street wall of the museum's Glassell School of Art on the opposite side of Montrose. The low tunnel vault that caps the office wing lends volumetric authority to the directionality of the street corridor. By Houston standards, Jiménez approached the back side of the building, where the surface parking lot is located, with a sense of *noblesse oblige*. He integrated cars into the architectural space of the Administration Building by claiming the parking lot as a foreground, rather than merely discarding it as beyond his realm of responsibility. Using the L-plan to shape outdoor space, Jiménez routed access to the rear entrance of the Administration Building through a concrete and granite-paved causeway, screened from the cars on one side by six transplanted magnolia trees. The breadth of this causeway and the height and full-bodied shape of the magnolia trees transform this passage from a wide sidewalk into an outdoor room. Paralleling the causeway is a separate entrance gallery serving the Glassell Junior School, which occupies the L-wing. Jiménez paired these redundant paths of circulation, letting them borrow from each other in order to amplify. Openings impart degrees of transparency and volumetric recession. Opposing interior and exterior stairs, glass canopies slung from metal rods, and the thick plate of the suspended canopy above the Junior School entrance loggia charge the overlap space of the magnolia terrace with their activating diagonals.

Inside the Administration and Junior School Building, Jiménez has fundamentally reconsidered the spatiality of the clerical workplace. Not only individual offices, but the central work stations and conference zones have access to natural light and views out. The continuity, and implied communal nature, of these broad, nave-like spaces are assured without sacrificing enclosure and definition for the work stations located there. On the first and second floors, Jiménez provides internal transom windows, so that the central spaces borrow natural light from the private offices (a technique that James Stirling & Michael Wilford employed in their alterations and additions to Anderson Hall at Rice University). This high sidelight emphasizes (without quite making one consciously aware of) the fact that spatial continuity is achieved at the plane of the ceiling. On the top floor, the ceiling of the central space is contoured to reflect the curvature of the roof vault. This volumetric configuration continues into the only work space permitted to overlap the Junior School wing, the museum's in-house graphic design studio, which unfolds as a single, unpartitioned space beneath the vault. Even staff members whose offices are in the basement remark on the lack of a feeling of confinement, due to Jiménez's Stirling & Wilford-like use of interior windows.

The Glassell Junior School is integrated so unostentatiously with the administrative offices that the social dimension of this conjunction is easily overlooked. Jiménez demonstrates how easily child care and education can be combined with the adult workplace, without compromise or interference. He spatializes this point in section. The second-floor studios of the Junior School reach up for north light, endowing the lower school wing with a profile that distinguishes it from the tunnel vault of the office building. On the back face of the building, this conjunction is architecturally resolved at the magnolia terrace through the agency of the activating diagonal.

The Museum of Fine Arts, like other public institutions in Houston, refers to its multi-building complex as a "campus." It is instructive to observe how Jiménez uses architecture to gently recall the museum to the intentions of its founders, which was to make the museum an integral part of the city rather than segregate it in an isolated enclave. The Administration and Junior School Building consistently opts for the city. It pulls together, rather than standing apart. It reshapes the workplace rather than merely cloaking it in external architectural novelties. It combines functions to produce a socially hybrid urban building rather than transforming hybridity into an arcane formal code.

In respect to its urban inclinations, the Administration and Junior School Building warrants comparison with the museum's most celebrated components, Mies's Brown Pavilion (1974) and Isamu Noguchi's Cullen Sculpture Garden (1986). All three seek to reinforce urban spatiality (which is to say, contained space), yet none fetishizes this intention or assumes it to be antithetical to modernism. By respecting the planning principles and geometry of the original museum building, Mies completed it with the regularly curved, steel framed, glass enclosed volume of the Brown Pavilion, which he used to provocatively spatialize the fractured curve of Bissonnet Avenue outside. Mies annexed exterior space along Bissonnet to hollow out a sidewalk-level passage, inset behind the massive steel columns of the Brown Pavilion. The pavilion's glass-walled gallery projects above this passage, enclosed yet transparent.

Noguchi used broken wall planes to spatially define the edges of Montrose and Bissonnet and, from inside the sculpture garden, visually delete cars to suggest that Houston is a garden city studded with significant buildings. Noguchi deployed the activating diagonal to "borrow" the prow-like edge of the adjacent Contemporary Arts Museum for the sculpture garden, and poetically condense an experience of the flat, slow-moving spatiality of Houston. Jiménez reciprocated with the chamfered wall plane at the Montrose entrance to the Administration and Junior School Building. This is the Administration Building's only overt acknowledgment of the Cullen Sculpture Garden, just as the limestone panels with which its exterior walls are faced are its only overt acknowledgment of the Brown Pavilion. Rather than conceiving his task as formulating a unifying campus style, Jiménez emulated Mies and Noguchi by making the Administration and Junior School Building shape urban space strongly yet uninsistently.

The Administration and Junior School Building also invites comparison with the nearby building of the Children's Museum of Houston (1992, Venturi, Scott-Brown & Associates and Jackson & Ryan). Critical attention has been focused almost exclusively on the postmodern propylaeum at the entrance to the Children's Museum and the Caryakids beneath its bus drop-off shelter. These imagistic elements represent an obvious contrast in attitude with Jiménez. Yet the rest of the Children's Museum suggests parallels in sensibility between Jiménez and Venturi & Scott-Brown. A link between Jiménez and Venturi & Scott-Brown is their mutual admiration for Nordic modernism (the rear elevation of the Junior School wing, in its balance of austerity and warmth, especially calls to mind the side chapels of Gunnar Asplund's Woodland Crematorium). Making architecture out of simple, defined shapes and radiant proportions--being good rather than being original, as Mies advocated--emerges as a strongly shared conviction. The rear elevation of the Administration Building and the rear elevation of the back building at the Children's Museum, with their horizontally elongated windows slotted beneath cowl-like projecting eaves lines, display a fascination with achieving ordinariness that scarcely registers yet subtly exalts.

An art-historical recognition of affinities would be misleading were it to suggest that Jiménez designs by reconfiguring other architects' works. His engagement with images differs from the imagistic borrowings of post-modern eclecticism. Jiménez has written about the power of images to impress memory and imagination. His dedication to poetry and film is bound up with the appeal of images. One senses that for Jiménez an extraordinary image is one that has the power to clarify, liberate, and emotionally move, like a religious icon is supposed to do. Architecture, because it is inhabited, is capable of spatializing the power of the image. The emotive intensity attributed to proportion is a way in which this spatializing power is conventionally addressed in architectural discourse. If one were forced to name just what it is that Jiménez's architecture is about, a likely response is: communicating through feeling. To the extent that Jiménez incorporates cultural narratives in his architecture they are secondary. His primary effort seems not to be to express conclusions, but to involve others in exploring the potential that architecture has to introduce experience. This intention may sound vague or arty. It perhaps seems insufficiently engaged theoretically, politically, or socially. What proves to be liberating in Jiménez's architecture is his consistent provision of conceptual free space. Discovering such spaces in buildings dedicated to production, such as the Fine Art Press, or to clerical work and education, such as the Administration and Junior School Building, is liberating in a culture that insists upon de-pressing the spaces of daily life in service to economic-determinist formulas. In cities with extensive historic fabric, older buildings often serve this liberating purpose simply because they were shaped by different circumstances. In Houston, with its thread-bare historic fabric, it is the rare new building that, as Wilhelm Hahn wrote of the Fine Art Press, "stands like a little outpost of faith beside its barbaric neighbors."

Given Jiménez's response to making architecture in Houston, where anything goes, it is intriguing to see how he responds when building outside Texas in circumstances that could not be more different from Houston. The W. L. S. Spencer Studio Art Building at Williams College in Williamstown, Massachusetts, affirms his commitment to respecting local circumstance. Yet it also displays his confidence in producing a building that formally is quite singular.

The campus of Williams College spreads out along the immaculate, rolling topography of Williamstown's Main Street. Its buildings are architecturally diverse. They tend to face Main Street frontally, surrounded by broad margins of turf. The college's dominant architectural language is based on its earliest building, West College of 1790, and consists of red brick blocks sparingly decorated with classical detail. (This neo-Georgian style was canonized by the Boston architects Cram, Goodhue & Ferguson during the 1910s and 1920s, the same years in which they designed Rice University in Houston.) Town buildings, faculty houses, and grandiose fraternity houses infiltrate among the college buildings. All adhere to the New England village tradition of free-standing construction and emphatic frontality with respect to the high street.

The Spencer Studio Art Building is not contextual, in the way that architecture is customarily described as being. Jiménez made no effort to conform to typological, stylistic, or material precedent at Williams. Instead, the Spencer Building is site specific, in the way that works of environmental art are characterized as being. Its planimetric configuration, spatial organization, and shaped profiles deliberately register external and internal pressures.

The building's site is peculiar, a shelf that is downhill from the nearest campus buildings (which back up to it), yet uphill from the town, including a bank and a church that face Main Street and unceremoniously abut the site with their parking lots. Because of its elevated height, the Spencer Studio Art Building is quite visible from the town, but not especially accessible. From the college's Berkeley Quadrangle, it is accessible but not especially visible.

The Spencer Studio Art Building appears from most prospects only in fragments, its first floor cut off by intervening buildings or rising topography. Jiménez seems to have conceived the building as a sequence of vignettes. The vista as one approaches from the Berkeley Quadrangle in the winter months is particularly compelling. The long west side of the building is a planar slab, sliced horizontally by staggered bands of slot windows that step right up to the fascia, emphasizing the fragile planarity of the wall without relying on the implication of one-point perspectival diminution that Jiménez's earlier treatment of the plane seemed to entail. The dark, slender trunks of a stand of mature trees on the steep downhill slope that cuts the Spencer Building off from the Berkeley Quadrangle figure against the light gray plane of its polished terrazzo block wall. This produces the kind of condensed cinematic image--biting and intense--that Jiménez prizes in the work of the Soviet film director Andrei Tarkovsky. The vantage point from which the Spencer Building can best be seen without obstruction is its south-facing "patio." It is for this prospect that Jiménez reserved an episode of architectural decoration--a gridded mosaic of windows, lead-coated copper panels, and red limestone revetment--above the arcade that opens off the ground-floor corridor. As one looks up at the second-floor windows from the courtyard, what the paneled grid frames is a view through the tutorial and painting studios and out the high north windows beneath the visor facing Main Street. Here, in the Berkshire Mountains of northwestern Massachusetts, the sky in the house reappears in Jiménez's architecture as a surprising visual epiphany.

These vignettes make one aware of how intently Jiménez was attuned to conditions at Williams, even though he did not defer to the Williams style. In the double-volume entrance vestibule, especially at the second-floor landing, one sees how Jiménez "inflected" (to use Robert Venturi's term) the building's corner entrance to frame-out all that wasn't Williams in order to visually assert a connection with the rest of the campus. There is something especially cinematic here about the way that he used framing not to construct a privileged vista (what one sees are the backs of dormitories in the Berkeley Quadrangle) but to establish a spatial identity by editing out.

Jiménez invests the interiors of the Spencer Building with a sense of spatial wit. He compares the double-volume sculpture workshop, which splits the building's section by being dropped below the ground floor as the site slopes down to the east, to an auto repair garage. Jiménez deflected this tall space, which fills the entire east wing of the building, into a parallelogram plan configuration in response to the site's skewed eastern property line. The third-floor drawing studio, in the southwest corner of the building, contains a sense of spatial mystery, achieved by encasing the fire stairs and ancillary spaces in a low-ceilinged annex, above which the high-set slot window visible on the west elevation, amid the trees, is recessed in section at an indeterminate distance from the studio's west interior partition. The set-back west window functions as a plane of light that illuminates the arc of the studio's ceiling. The snappy visor that diagonally activates the Spencer Building's north elevation can even be seen as contextual: a salute to Williamstown's most famous modern architectural landmark, Marcel Breuer's Robinson House of 1947.

The Spencer Studio Art Building is not as ingratiating as the Central Administration and Glassell Junior School Building. From outside, it feels aloof and self-contained (perhaps as a result of Jiménez's decision to raise the sill levels of north-facing ground-floor windows, so that those in the printing studio would not have to look at the faculty, bank, and church parking lots). A comparison of these two buildings raises the issue of character in Jiménez's architecture: how architecture--especially modern architecture--represents differences in situation, purpose, and prestige. The Houston building is a *palazzo*, a public building, even though it is just an office building. The Williamstown building is a *taller* (which in Spanish can mean studio but carries the connotation of workshop), even though it is part of a well-known institution and can be seen from Main Street. The Spencer Studio Building has been impressed with a sense of complex ordinariness. Slender dashes of red limestone imbue the building's placid gray surfaces with a nervous energy, hinting at the creative work that transpires there. The diagonal visor capping the grid of north windows seems to channel the clear light of inspiration into the luminous volumes within. Although the Spencer Building can accommodate the public, its dedication is to those who come to make, work, and learn. It derives its architectural character from fulfilling this purpose.

Jiménez's most recent designs for public buildings--the proposed Art League of Houston Building and a branch bank prototype for the Irwin Union Bank and Trust Company in Columbus, Indiana--demonstrate his continued exploration of architectural themes meaningful to him. In Houston, on a site two blocks from his studio compound, he has designed the Art League Building as an urban wall plane activated by a rising diagonal. The Irwin Union Bank, Jiménez's first major commercial building commission (although it too is implicated in the art connection: he was referred to the bank's chairman, William Irwin Miller, by the Minneapolis collectors Mr. and Mrs. Kenneth N. Dayton), develops themes posited in the Drive-In Library project.

Since beginning his practice in 1983 at age 24, Jiménez has pursued architectural interests that set him apart from the polemics and personalities of U.S. architecture during the 1970s, '80s, and '90s. Neither postmodern eclecticism nor its successors have engaged him. Instead, Jiménez has consistently sought to shape architecture capable of imparting to its occupants, in the midst of their daily lives, access to spatial experiences that possess an other, unspecifiable dimension. In modern art and architectural discourse, this dimension is most frequently named the spiritual. It is a term that one applies with reluctance to Jiménez's architecture, as much for its trite connotations as for its lack of specificity.

Jiménez's desire to emphasize and represent this dimension spatially derives from his cultural experiences as a Latin American. To the extent that U.S. architectural culture reflects mainstream cultural models grounded in marketing and competition, with their tendency to deform principled positions into popularity contests between products and celebrities, Jiménez has elected to keep his distance. What he offers the occupants of his buildings as an architectural corrective is an implied spatial invitation: to feel deeply, to reflect intensely, to live passionately and wisely. The attributes of Jiménez's spaces--the static plane, the activating diagonal, abstracted views, acoustic resonance, the entrancing image, ecstatic color, imaginary space--demonstrate architecture's capacity for what might be called the spiritual edification of its inhabitants. The sky in the house is a poignant symbol of this phenomenon. It is an apparition that moves you by revealing the power of architecture to disclose the world.

*Stephen Fox is a Fellow of the Anchorage Foundation of Texas.*

# Jiménez Studio & House

1983-1993

Houston, Texas

The four buildings that comprise the house and studio complex represent an incremental and ongoing process of design and construction that started in 1983.  The initial project consisted of two single volume structures placed opposite one another on one-half of a 50 by 100 feet lot, linked by a tall wooden fence and a courtyard between them.  The two concrete masonry buildings established a territory of total privacy where work and living activities formed one interwoven entity.  In 1986, a third and larger structure was added on the remaining half of the lot.  Situated 60 feet from its street property line, the two-story building became the principal and most private studio space.  Subsequent alterations of both interior and  exterior spaces have underlined the flexibility inherent in the simple forms that compose the complex.  Adaptable and interchangeable, these forms do not render the architecture obsolete, but permit volumetric and spatial variations.

In 1993, a fourth building was constructed across the street on a similar sized lot. The 1,600 square foot house overlooks the studio compound, extending the domain of the latter.  From the street, the house is essentially a two-story wall facing north, protecting a large garden behind it. The large window at the center of this wall infuses both interior levels with an ample and gentle quality of light.  Continuing the spatial concerns of the studio complex, the house consists of a pure volume subdivided by partial and corner walls, defining varying conditions of privacy and light.  The compactness and simplicity of the house, with its solid and eco-nomical construction, and its luminous interiors, aim to introduce a new possible prototype for the area and in turn to establish an urban reference for the future.

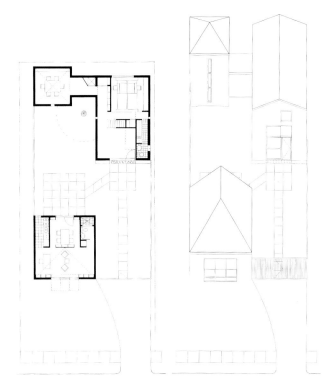

*left* :
Site plan and axonometric

*below* :
View of studio complex and
courtyards

*right* :
West light animates two-story
volume of main studio

Main studio spatial transformations
(left to right): 1986, 1989, 1990

*above* :
Main studio stair detail

*right* :
Jimenez's personal studio

*below* :
Street elevation of house from studio
complex entrance

*right* :
Incremental changes and additions:
1983, 1986, 1990, 1993

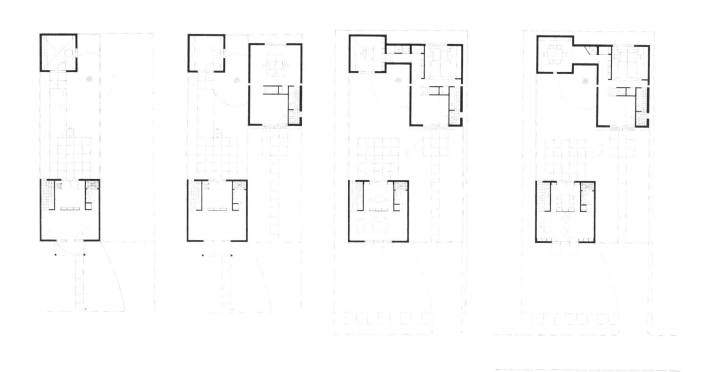

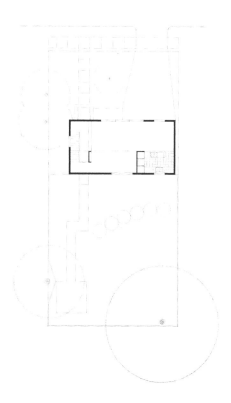

# Houston Fine Art Press

1985-1987
Houston, Texas

The site chosen for this printing workshop was a 39 by 300 feet sliver of land in one of Houston's industrial zones. The design solution demonstrates the viability of such residual pieces of urban space. The building workshop is a steel frame structure infilled with plastered concrete block walls on its exterior. It is a continuous volume divided into two adjacent individual areas. The larger space includes a vaulted ceiling that hovers over the printing presses. The smaller space has a vaulted ceiling and provides offices and a gallery.

A spatial progression through the building begins with its most public functions (curatorial and offices) along a gallery of windows framing a grass courtyard. It terminates in its most private and insular functions (printing, storage, photo rooms). Midway through this programmatic sequence a directional shift and scale change occurs. The shifted axis is oriented toward the mezzanine and its narrow stairway. This space accommodates a graphic arts work area and a balcony that overlooks the entire length of the building.

As a constant and unifying component in the design, a series of north windows and clerestories extend the length of the building, infusing the volume with a subtle and serene light. A walled-in parking and courtyard area interlocks with the building, creating a self-sufficient enclave and an architectural whole.

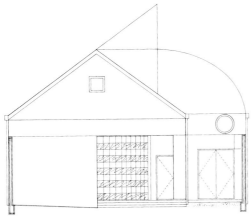

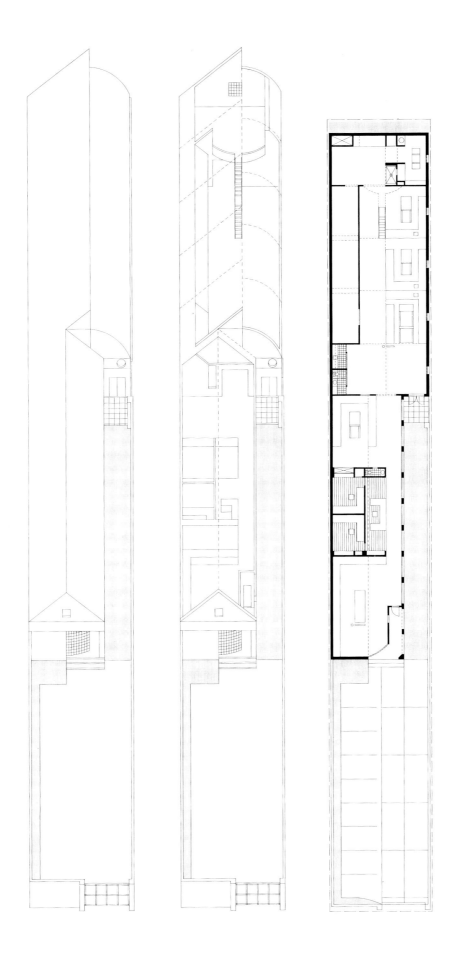

# Lynn Goode Gallery

1990-1991

Houston, Texas

The Lynn Goode Gallery is located in a mixed-use neighborhood known as Houston's Gallery Corridor. The two-story wood frame and stucco structure is defined by three existing oak trees. The 4,500 square foot building incorporates gallery spaces varied in area and height within the limits prescribed by these towering trees.

A central stairway simultaneously divides and integrates the exhibition spaces. It is also a platform bridge where visitors can look over the various display walls as well as the framed vistas of the tree branches. The constant vistas unveil subtle changes of light and season throughout the year, contrasting with the changing cycle of exhibitions.

The gallery is not solely a container for works of art but also a space that enhances the experience of looking at art. Thus the spatial unfolding aims to create both a feeling of expansiveness and intimacy as one moves from one space to another. The natural light, mostly from the east and the north, enters the space filtered by the sheltering trees. An enclosed court-yard has been included in the design as a sculpture garden, a place of total privacy interrupted only by the rustle and shadow of the oak branches across the bright stucco walls.

*right* :
North / front elevation

*above* :
View from second floor looking
north

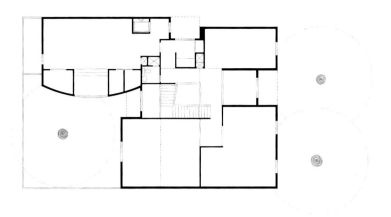

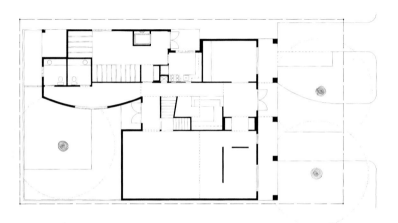

*left* :
First and second floor plans

*below* :
Sectional model through main
gallery space

*right* :
Two-story entry vestibule

# Drive-In Library

1990-1991

The 4,000 square foot library is a drive-in prototype that can be placed at various sites throughout the city. The masonry and aluminum clad structure is a roadside building which functions much like a drive-in bank or gas station. The prototype is both an independent pavilion and a free-standing sign that might be found along a freeway underpass, an intersection, or at the corner of a strip center parking lot.

Books can be checked out via the drive-in tellers, or they can be obtained inside the building. Three individual reading rooms are provided on the ground floor and a two-story volume at the upper floor for both reading and book display. An underground book storage/vault services both levels and the teller stations.

The drive-in prototype aims to facilitate the transaction and accessibility of books at each particular setting. It aspires to be both marker and cultural presence along its ever shifting urban landscape.

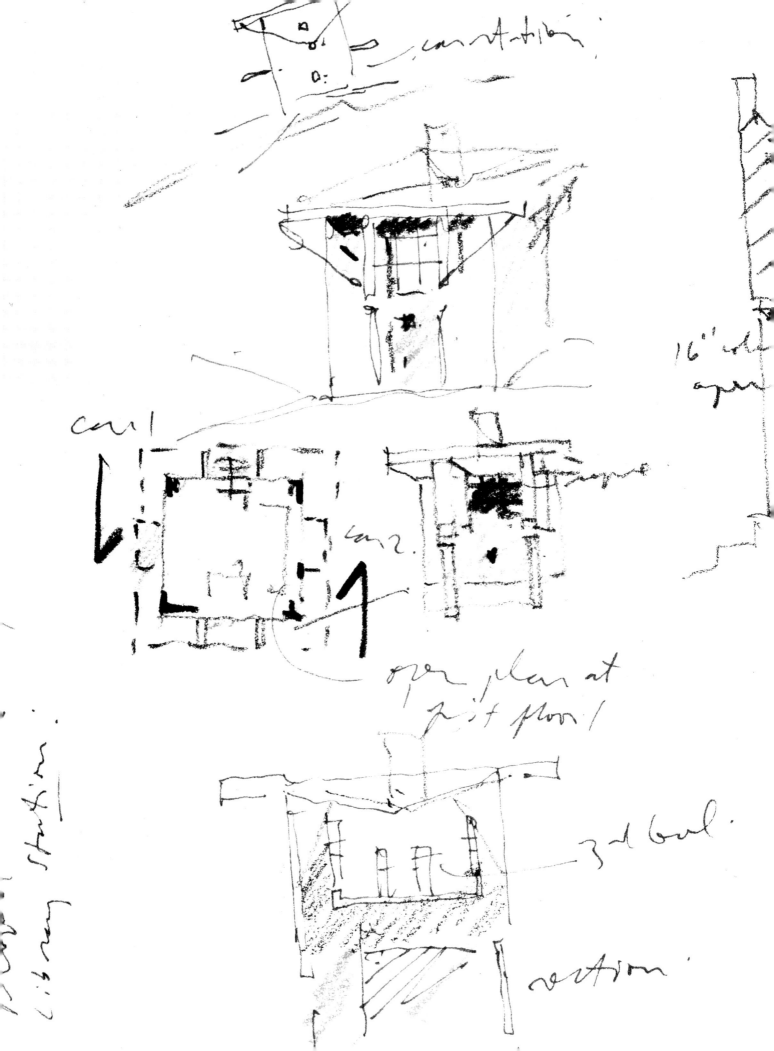

construction

16" old
open

can 1

can 2.

open plan at
first floor

3rd level.

section.

library situation.

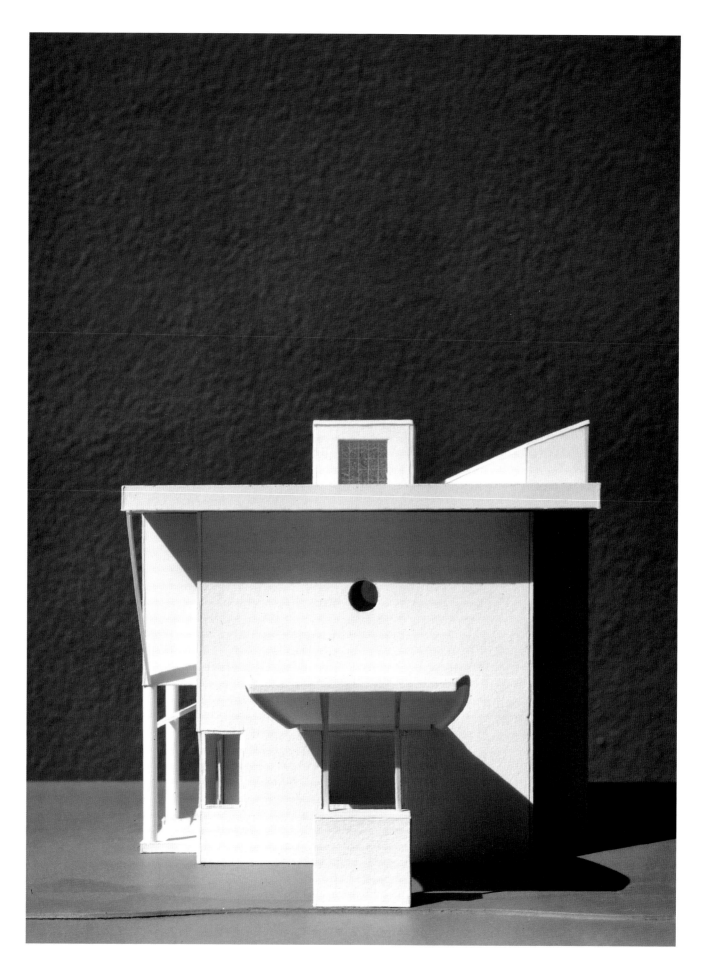

*left* :
Drive-In side elevation

*right* :
First and second floor plan

*below right* :
Front elevation

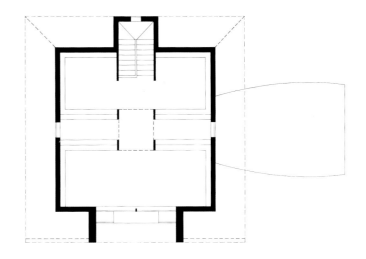

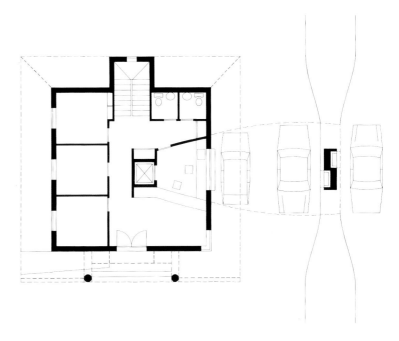

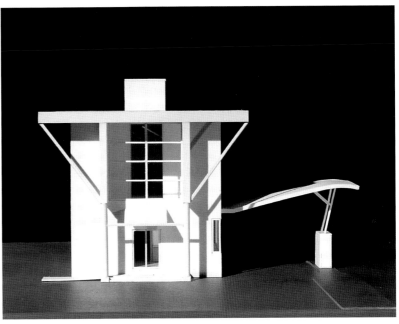

# Central Administration and Junior School Museum of Fine Arts, Houston

1991-1994

Houston, Texas

The Central Administration and Junior School Building is part of a master plan set out by the Museum of Fine Arts for its future, incremental expansion. Rather than locating all of the museum expansion requirements into one structure, the museum opted for individual buildings with specific programs linked to one another in the manner of a campus complex. The museum's original structure and its two subsequent extensions by Mies van der Rohe are to remain as the centerpiece and common reference for all of the other buildings that compose the master plan.

The design solution for the 60,000 square foot building consists of an L-shaped plan that integrates and identifies the dual function of its program. The administrative offices (Development, Accounting, Personnel, Marketing, Publications and Graphics, and Education among them) and the Junior School form two clearly defined wings joined by a light filled central lobby. Each of the two wings has its own entryway. The layout of the interior spaces reinforces the museum's desire to have a flexible plan. All of the offices as well as the studio classrooms are within a modular and repetitive system which can be altered to permit future spatial changes, if needed.

The building's placement on the site preserves as many of the existing oak trees as possible along the main thoroughfare, Montrose Boulevard. The main building elevation stretches the length of the property to create with the adjacent trees a protected canopy and a public promenade along Montrose. The parking spaces in the back of the building are defined by a borderline of newly planted oak and magnolia trees.

The principal materials of the building: limestone, anodized aluminum panels, galvanized steel roofing panels, insulated glass, glass block walls, granite pavers and terrazzo floors, combine to establish both subtle and direct references to the other museum buildings and gardens, while asserting a new contribution to the museum's ongoing history.

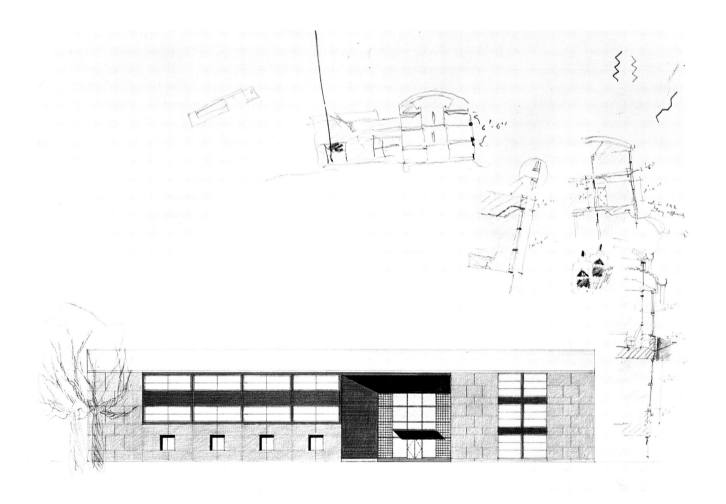

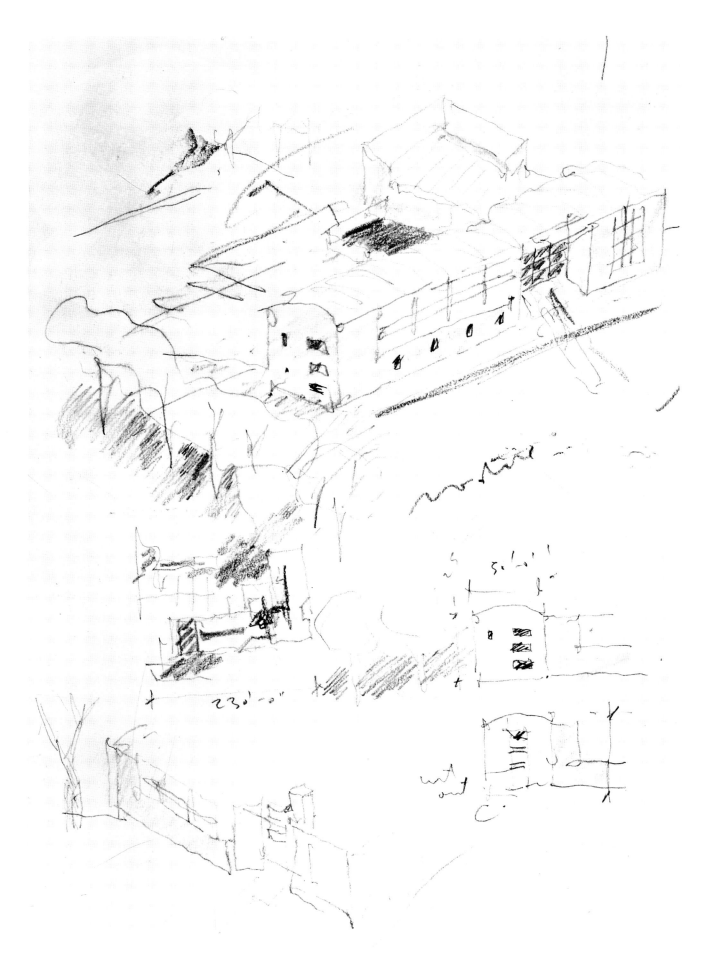

*below* :
Site model with view of building's
west elevation

*right* :
First, second, and third floor plans

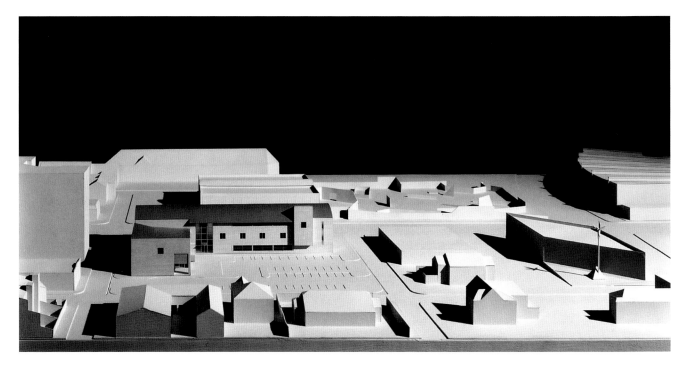

*below* :
Site model with view of building's
west elevation

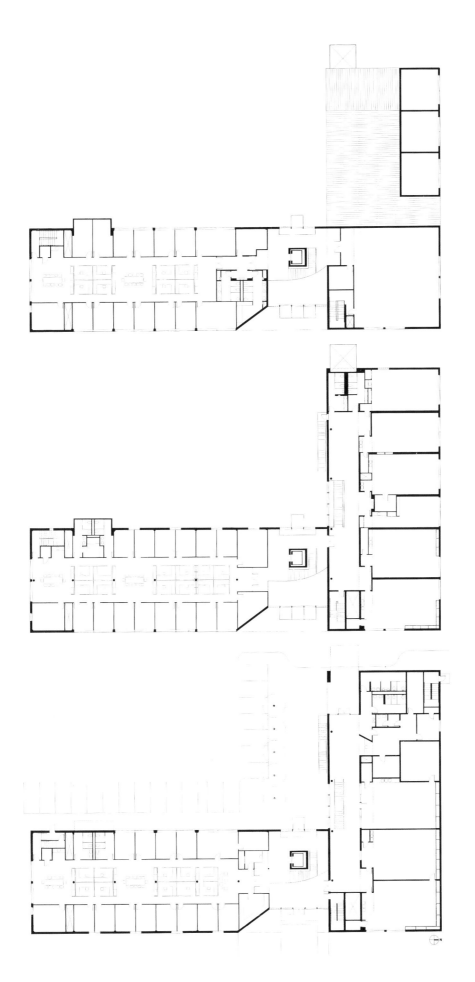

*below* :
South elevation

*right* :
Section through the three-story
lobby, section through the
administrative offices, and the
south elevation

80

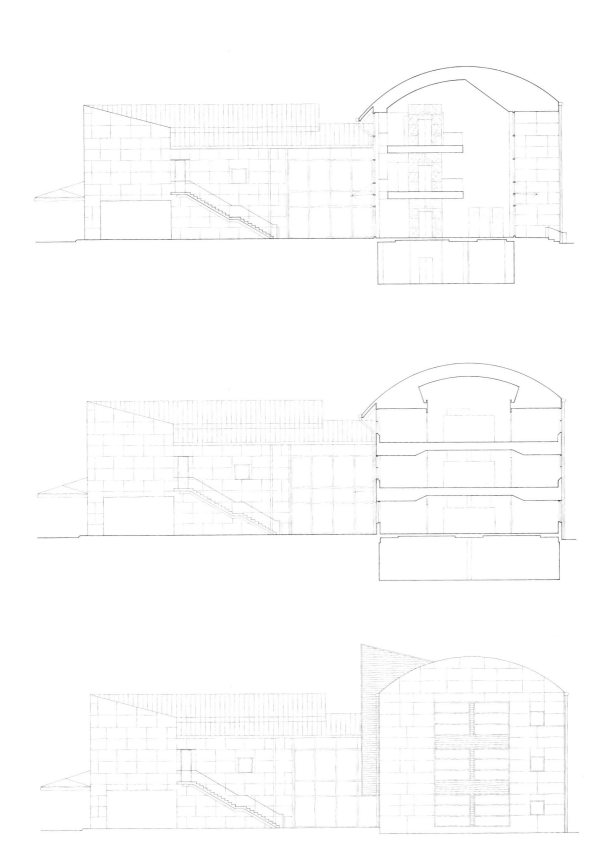

*above & right*:
Views of the lobby stairway and
elevator enclosure

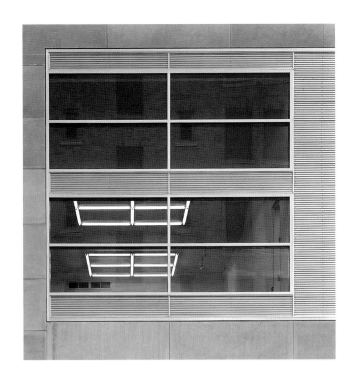

*above* :
Open offices and adjacent private
offices on the third floor

*right* :
Main entrance to administrative
offices from main lobby

# Art League of Houston

1994-1996

Houston, Texas

The Art League of Houston is a 9,000 square foot building facing Montrose Boulevard, one of Houston's most diverse and active thoroughfares. The new design replaces the institution's existing buildings on the site, a group of three inefficient and congested wood houses enclosing a common courtyard. A metal shed added several years ago to the east will remain as a multipurpose space.

The design solution separates the two main programmatic functions (studios and gallery), placing them opposite one another and linking them by a common circulation and entrance median. The building extends to the maximum allowable construction setback limits to maximize the longitudinal use of the site. Circulation becomes an extension of the gallery and entry, enlarging the spatial qualities of each of the two programmatic functions. A courtyard is integral to the composition: a public space, a sculpture garden, and a temporary exhibition area. The building wraps around this open space.

The parking zone, framed by a row of densely planted oak trees, parallels the full length of the building's west elevation. This wall of trees filters the intense west light and heat, providing shade along Montrose to the minimally fenestrated west elevation. The parking zone becomes a garden rather than the ever-present glaring concrete voids found everywhere in the city. The steel framed structure is to be infilled with concrete block masonry units finished with a smooth stucco coating, aluminum window units, galvanized steel roofing and wall panels, concrete floors, and industrial plywood.

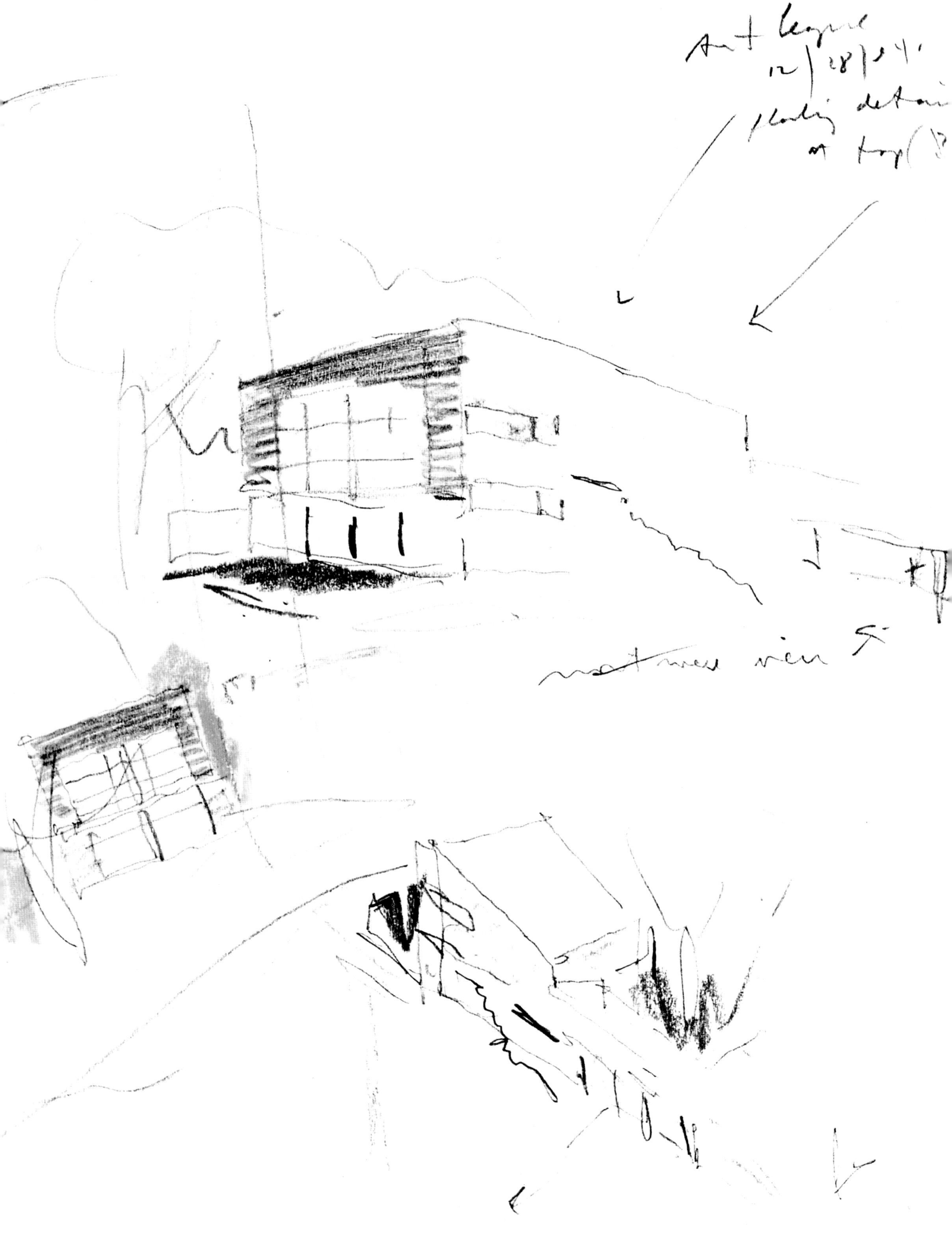
Art League
12/28/94

*below & below right* :
Model views

*Right* :
North elevation

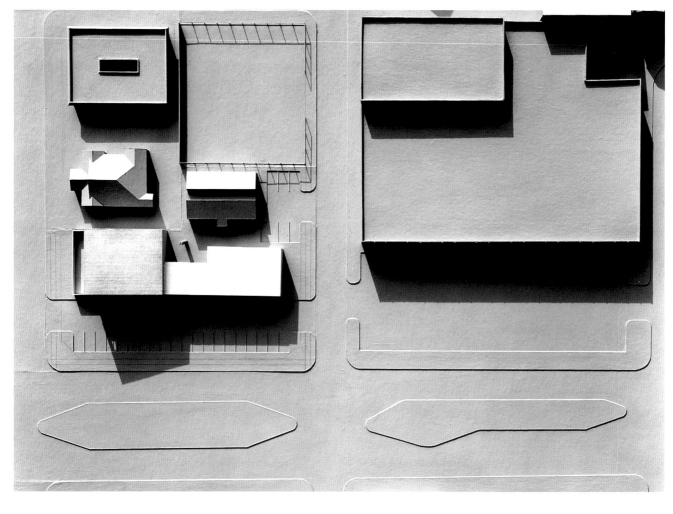

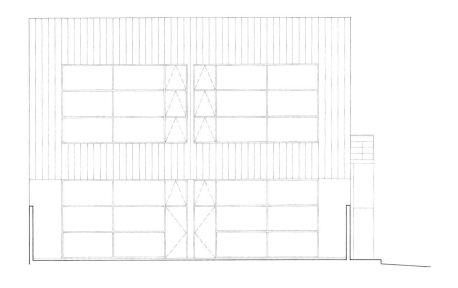

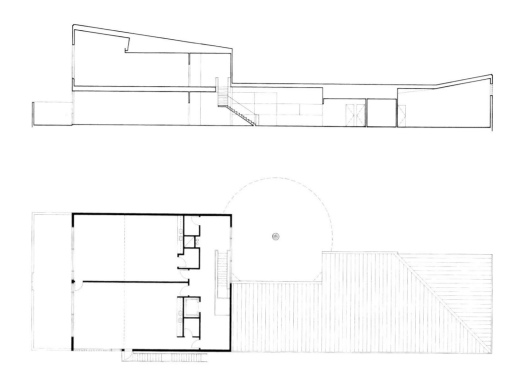

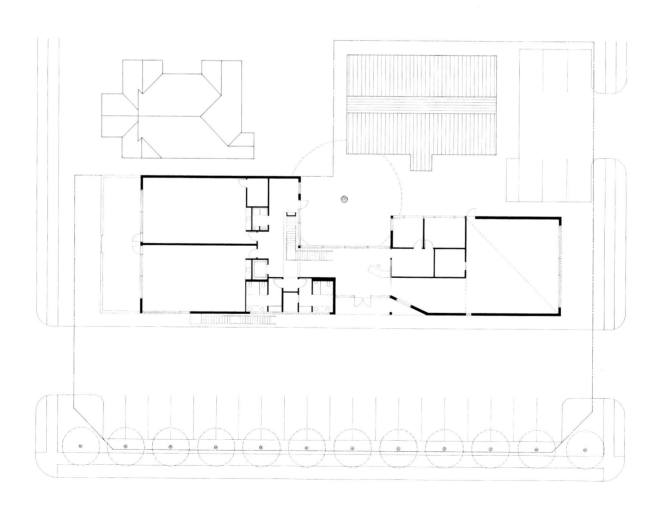

# Irving Union Bank Prototype

1995-1996

Columbus, Indiana

The Irwin Union Bank, its headquarters originally designed by Eero Saarinen in the mid-1950's, has, as it has grown, inserted various  branches in Columbus and its vicinity.  The bank's continued growth has generated a need for a branch prototype that can easily adapt to the demands of new markets, unforeseen site conditions, and changing banking programs.  The 4,000 square foot bank branch is a prototype that aims  to maximize both spatial flexibility, site and technological adaptability.  The square plan has a central vaulted space where open offices are located.  This space is both a banking hall and an interchangeable office layout, and an open container receiving natural light from both ends of its continuous arc.

 All other banking activities such as tellers, vaults, and private offices wrap around this central area, creating a peripheral ring.  The plan can be rotated or altered to respond to programmatic fluctuations by switching the principal components of the design.  For instance, if a specific site requires it, the drive-in teller's metal canopy, which pivots from one of the four building walls, can be positioned to hinge from the opposite wall.

The design also aims to achieve a balance between two types of banking: the personal one-to-one relationship between banker and customer, and the more expedient transaction offered by the drive-in tellers.  Two distinct roof forms highlight this difference while asserting their interdependence.

 A steel framed structure infilled with concrete masonry units, the branch bank will have a smooth stucco finish exterior with interwoven lead coated copper panels, interior finishes are a combination of warm woods, industrial carpet, and applied color accenting what will be predominantly a multi-hued white volume.

*left* :
Section through central bank space

*below* :
Rear elevation of bank

*right* :
Mid-section through bank drive-in
teller area and offices, floor plan,
and front elevation

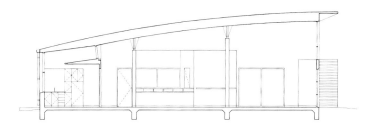

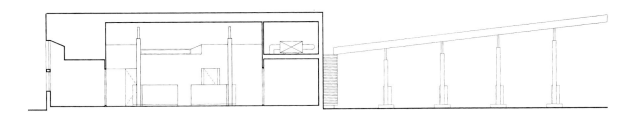

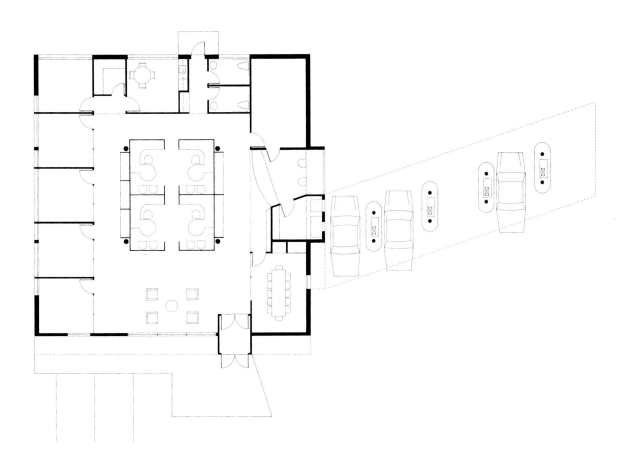

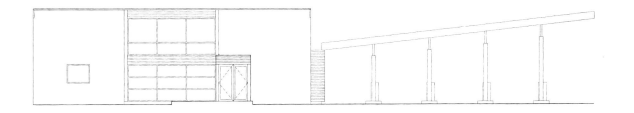

# Spencer Studio Art Building
# Williams College

1993-1996

Williamstown, Massachusetts

The 37,000 square foot building consolidates various studio spaces scattered throughout the college into a single structure. Although situated on a peripheral site at the farthest southeast section of the campus, the new art building enjoys astonishing views of the surrounding Berkshire Mountains. The design aims to maximize these views and to integrate them as a vital component of the life of the art studios.

The building is a partial U-shape that interlocks with two courtyards. One is small and bracketed by the building's two wings; the other radiates from its center towards a wall of tall, dense trees creating a large court garden. The latter will be a constant display of the exuberant color changes present in these trees throughout the year.

The studios are distributed according to different requirements for natural light and height. The lower level contains the photography and video studios in a partially buried section. Printmaking, intaglio printing, and the sculpture studios, which require a higher ceiling and volumetric sections, are placed along the slope of the site. The upper floors contain the remainder studios and faculty offices. The entry vestibule, the student gallery, and the seminar room are located adjacent to the pivot-like corner of the building. This three-story open volume, the building's center and common link, is occupied by an open steel and concrete step stairway. The main purpose of the design is to establish an active place for making art, one that is cognizant of its private and public realms and that allows students to discover their individual pursuits within spaces that include the majesty of the nearby mountains.

The building's plan and volumetric shape are fit within a difficult and contained site. Thus the plan recontours the site to maximize the space use. The roof forms extend the site's slope and the profiles of the surrounding mountains.

*below* :
Model view of west elevation

*right* :
Partial view of north elevation

102

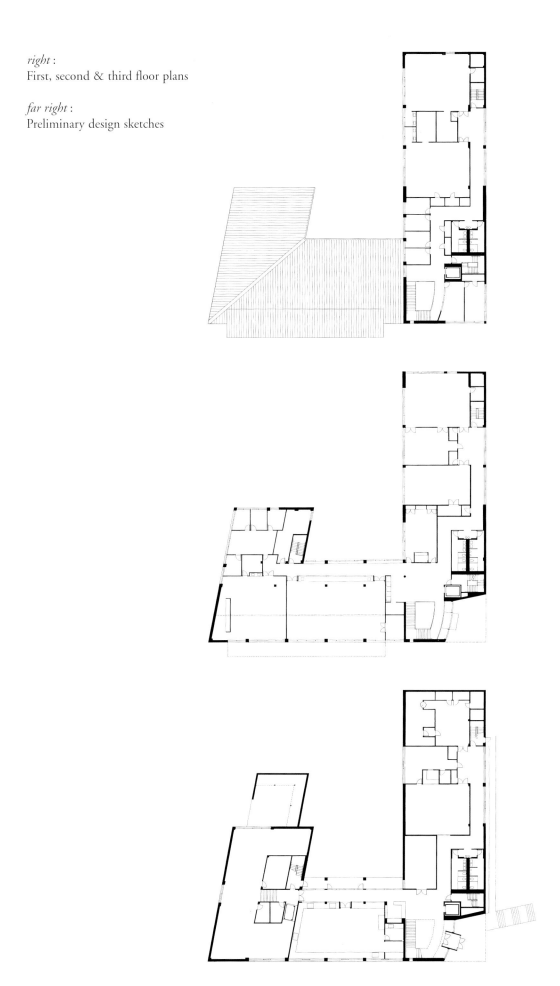

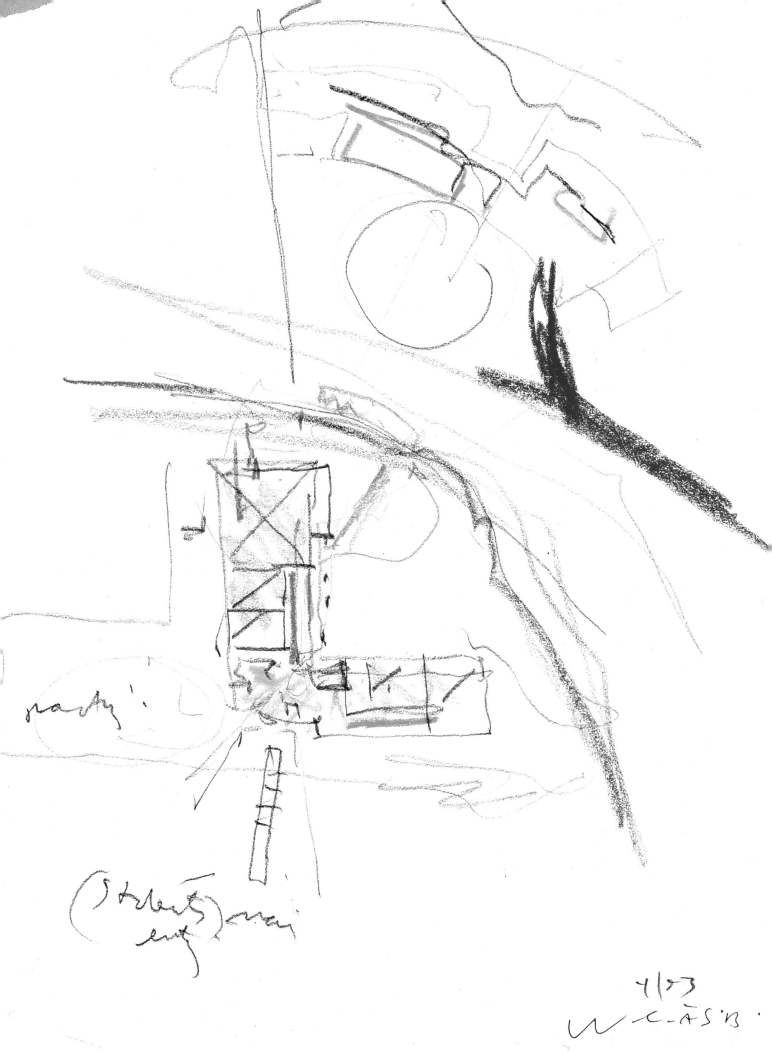

*below* :
North elevation

*right* :
Canopy detail over north elevation

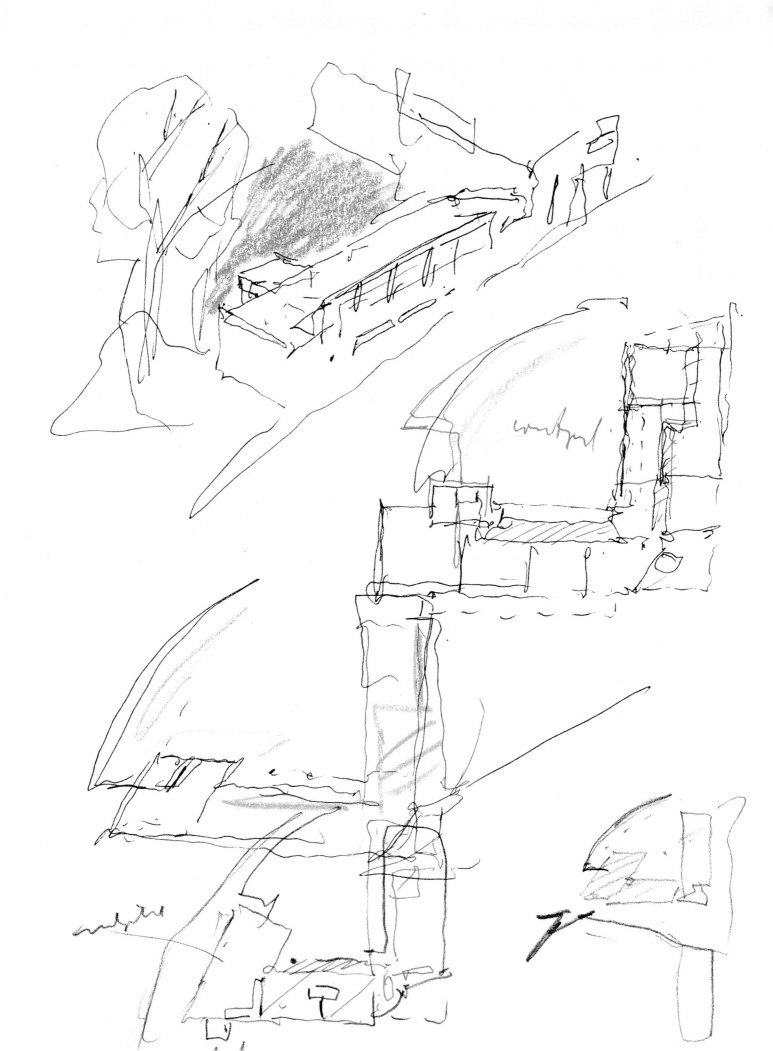

*below* :
Main lobby at second floor

*right* :
Student gallery seen from stair
landing

*left* :
Section through main lobby
and upper & lower studios

*below & right* :
Views and details of the
three-story lobby

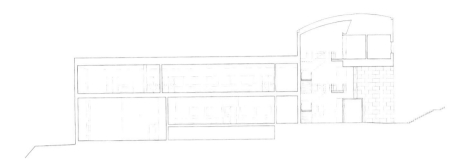

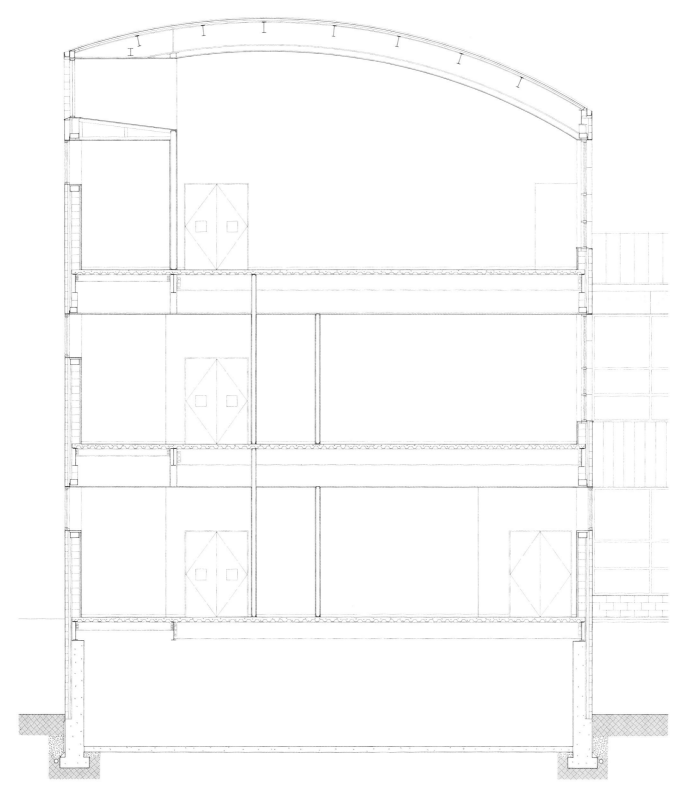

121

# On Architecture At Rice,
# Carlos Jiménez, Urbanism and Volcanoes
*Lars Lerup*

Over the last three years, *Architecture at Rice* has published books along two seemingly disparate trajectories: one that we may call *operational* and the other *plastic*. Thus, Rem Koolhaas' **Conversation with Students** and Albert Pope's **Ladders** belong in the former, while Carlos Jiménez's **Buildings** and **Stanley Saitowitz** belong to the latter category. Yet, this bifurcation is too simplistic, when in Saitowitz's case one recognizes his work as an *artificial geography*, and even more clearly in Jiménez's case, in his work's distinct commitment to *urbanism.*

The relationship between the operational and urbanism is intimate. Simply put, the plastically inclined architect's work is ultimately turned inward, deeply self-referential, while urbanist architects unfailingly see their work in part as a *gift to the street* -- put there to motivate public life, to set the city into operation. At Rice the intense interest in urbanism is recent, yet the interest reaches far back to the almost forgotten subject of *urban design* and and to the *architecture of the city*. In its last return, the architecture of the city can be traced back some thirty years with the occurrence of Aldo Rossi's writings. His connection with Carlos Jiménez's is in turn visible in all his buildings.[1] Most notably in what one may call *the blank stare* of the facade with its figures of windows, doors and wall set inside the typological (and topological) horizon of the *House* or the *Building*, in turn set against **The Blue of the Sky**.[2] The stare is loaded with the city's radical separation between the public (invested in a populated street) and the private (invested in an inscrutable facade). Jiménez's urbanism is not flaunted by breaking the suburban or campus setback rules to hark back to the long lost perimeter block, but compressed or blatantly lacking. This compression or lack of diverts the blankness of the stare, investing it with a certain intensity -- like a volcano waiting to erupt.

In his own house, the customary living room window has been "kicked upstairs", and left a blank wall behind that is doubly blind by conspicuously lacking the ubiquitous garage door -- in fact, the garage as been kicked-out of the house. This bi-pedal action drives the car back into the street (or eliminates it in favor of the pedestrian?). The switching of night and day activities, indicated by the migrating window, elevates the awake dweller above the vast flatness of the Houstonian ground plane (in contra-distinction to the sleeping dweller, now safely in bed on the ground floor), pushing everyday life into the omnipresent zohemic canopy. Like Calvino's **Baron in the Trees**, the Jiménezes have joined the winged creatures, one step closer to *the blue of the sky*. Here Jiménez unleashes energies, usually reined-in by the tight rules of the mortgage controlled single-family house. These pent-up energies distend the house beyond the borders of its tranquilized position as an investment or symbol of Home into the realm of urbanism. The dilation is made ever more explosive by the house being on axis with and across the street from his architectural studio, eliminating the commute between house and work. (After all, Houstonians collectively spend 35 years every day in commuting.) Jiménez's short-hand urbanism, confined to the menu of the facade, opens the files on "how should we live in a zohemic city," and "what will happen to the commute (and all its assorted paraphernalia) when we all work at home?" suggesting that once the volcano erupts, our ways and means of life will too.

Susan Sontag's *Cavaliere*, the subject in her recent book **The Volcano Lover**, has an eerily cool regard for the violent Vesuvius, yet his passion for the furnace itself burns white-hot. The Cavaliere's collection of various specimens, often perilously compiled under eruption, are assembled with an Englishman's cool. Yet one can sense that the apparent fastidiousness rests on a deep passion that in itself is both unruly and obsessive. Jiménez's relation to his work (his secluded personal design cell away from the din of the rest of his studio) and to architecture (his extensive collection of books) divulge a similar cool passion that occasionally threatens to break the silence: a brightly colored facade in his studio; the missing door in an otherwise proper house facade; or just waiting for Houston's movie industry, the ice-cold white entry and stair space in the Museum Administration Building (juxtaposed to the dripping hot summer night) --the *mise-en-scene* of a deathly chase leading beyond to some unseen yet expected end of the architectural promenade.

> *Sade worried about satiety; he could not conceive of passion without provocation. The Cavaliere did not worry about running out of feeling. For him the volcano was a stimulus for contemplation. Noisy as Vesuvius could be, it offered something like what he experienced with his collections. Islands of silence.*[3]

Stephen Fox, Houston's unofficial City Historian (and very possibly its Last Pedestrian), situates Carlos Jiménez's work in the extended architectural and urban geography of Houston and beyond, revealing the rich fabric of the Museum District, peppered with buildings that like volcanoes, more or less active, peak out of the otherwise indistinct undergrowth of an ever-changing *Mittellandschaft*. The landscape surrounding Volcanoes is in part the result of the latter, yet in Houston this figurative spawning has to date only resulted in more volcanoes. Some of the first begun by the Menils. However, Carlos Jiménez's persistent practice may in the very long run not only inflect the Middle Landscape, but help to bend the physico-social aspects of the equation of house, home, institution and work place, to create a new volcanic landscape.

Yet Jiménez's work is not just read-only urbanist menus, but plastico-volcanic articulations that push and pull at our gaze, rub against our bodies, and fill our nostrils -- the material of the architect's world (*the cultural and visceral surplus*) that the operational so vigorously denies.

> *The mountain provided a different experience from anything else, a different measure.  The land has spread, the sky has grown, the gulf has widened. You don't have to remember who you are.*[4]

**Notes**

[1] Made indirectly more apparent by Rafael Moneo's presence in this book, since he wrote the most seminal essays "On Typology" and "On Aldo Rossi" in the long gone **Oppositions** 5 and 11.

[2] Aldo Rossi, "The Blue of the Sky" in **Oppositions** 5, (IAUS and MIT Press, Cambridge: 1976) pp.31-34.

[3] Susan Sontag, **The Volcano Lover: A Romance**, (Vintage, London: 1993) p.32.

[4] ibid. p.57.

# CARLOS JIMENEZ

- Born in San Jose, Costa Rica (1959)
- Moved to the United States (1974)
- University of Houston, College of Architecture (1977-81)
- Established own studio in Houston (1982)

## AWARDS

**1996**
- Favrot Chair in Architecture, Tulane University, New Orleans
- "Record Houses" Award, Architectural Record Magazine

**1995**
- "Forty Under Forty", New York

**1994**
- "Emerging Voices", The Architectural League of New York
- "Record Houses" Award, Architectural Record Magazine

**1990**
- "Record Houses" Award, Architectural Record Magazine

**1988**
- "Young Architects", The Architectural League of New York

**1987**
- "Young Architects", Progressive Architecture Magazine

**1981**
- "Best Thesis Award" and "Best Portfolio Award", College of Architecture,University of Houston

## VISITING PROFESSORSHIP

- TULANE UNIVERSITY,  New Orleans (1996)
- GRADUATE SCHOOL OF DESIGN, Harvard University (1996)
- UNIVERSITY OF NAVARRA, E.T.S.A.N., Pamplona, Spain (1995)
- WILLIAMS COLLEGE, Williamstown, Massachusetts (1994)
- UNIVERSITY OF HOUSTON, (1991, 1994)
- UNIVERSITY OF TEXAS, Arlington (1990-1996)
- SCI-ARC, Los Angeles (1990, 1991)
- UNIVERSITY OF CALIFORNIA LOS ANGELES (1990)
- TEXAS A & M UNIVERSITY, College Station (1987, 1989)
- RICE UNIVERSITY, Houston (1987, 1994)

## EXHIBITIONS

**1996**
- "Carlos Jimenez: Three Buildings", Tulane University School of Architecture, New Orleans
- "Condition of the Aperture:  Buildings by Carlos Jimenez", Williams College Museum of Art, Williamstown, Massachusetts

**1994**
- "Carlos Jimenez:  Four Projects", Chang Gallery, Kansas State University, College of Architecture and Design
- "Intervented Spaces", Museo de Arte Carrillo Gil, Mexico City
- "Best Laid Plans", Lawndale Art and Performance Center, Houston
- "Two Museum Additions", The Architectural League of New York
- "Five Architects: Five Buildings in Texas", The University of Texas at Austin, School of Architecture

**1992**
- "The Architect's Sketchbook:  Current Practice", Canadian Center of Architecture, Montreal

**1991**
- "Contemporary Architectural Drawings", Wallach Gallery, Buel Center, Columbia University, New York
- "Texas/Mexico Architecture", University of Texas at San Antonio

**1990**
- "The Sketchbook and Contemporary Practice", The Getty Center for the History of Art and  the Humanities, Santa Monica
- "Project Houston", Diverse Works Gallery, Houston
- "Carlos Jimenez:  Four Projects", Perloff Hall, University of California Los Angeles
- "U.S.A./U.S.S.R. 1980-1990 Urban Projects", New York/Moscow

**1988**
- "Hypothesis", Urban Center Gallery, The Architectural League of New York

**1982**
- "Explorations:  Houston", Museum of Finnish Architecture, Helsinki

## WRITINGS

-"Some Remarks about Travel, Pamplona, and a Studio Project",
MEMORIA DE PROYECTOS 2, E.T.S.A.N., University of Navarra,
1996
-"Fisherman's House, Conca dei Marini (1929), The Travel Sketches of
Louis I. Kahn", WILLIAMS COLLEGE MUSEUM OF ART,
Williamstown, 1996
-"Some Observations and one building", OZ, Journal of the College of
Architecture and Design, Kansas State University, Vol. 17, 1995
-"Un Poeta de la Luz: Luis Barragan", EL PAIS, Madrid, Nov. 26, 1994
-"A moment for celebration and caution", UNIVERSITY DEL
DISENO, Catalogue, San Jose, Costa Rica, 1994
-"Between Dallas and Fort Worth - An Unforseen Journey", RECENT
ARCHIVES, University of Texas-Arlington, School of Architecture, 1994
-"Horizontes Tejanos: Donald Judd y la Fundacion Chinati",
ARQUITECTURA VIVA, No. 34, Madrid, January-February, 1994
-"Reflections from the Eye of the Storm", A+U, Tokyo, December, 1993
-"The Drawing on the Wall, Tadao Ando at the Menil Collection",
CITE, No. 28, Houston, 1992
-"El Hotel de la Pradera", ARQUITECTURA VIVA, No. 21, Madrid,
November -December, 1991
-"Cuarto de Costura, Morphosis: Tienda y Exposicion Leon Max",
AQUITECTURA VIVA, No. 16, Madrid, January - February, 1991
-"El Guardian de la Memoria", ARQUITECTURA VIVA, No. 14,
Madrid, September-October, 1990
-"Jimenez Studio, Summer 1990", SCI-ARC NEWSLETTER No. 4,
Southern California Instiute of Architecture, Santa Monica, August -
September, 1990
-"The Echo of Freeways", QUADERNS D'ARQUITECTURA I
URBANISME, No.184, Barcelona, January-March, 1990
-"A Conversation with Aldo Rossi", CITE, Houston, Spring, 1990
-"A Brooding Peninsular Light: Eric Gunnar Asplund's Drawings at
Farish Gallery", CITE, Houston, Fall, 1989
-"Legend of Sky and Earth", EXPLORATION-HOUSTON, Exhibition
Catalogue, Finnish Architecture Museum, Helsinki, 1982

## SELECTED BIBLIOGRAPHY

**1996**
-"DICTIONNAIRE DE L'ARCHITECTURE MODERNE ET CON-
TEMPORAINE", Editions Hazan/Institute Francais D'Architecture,
Paris
-Papademetriou, Peter, "Loose Fit: The Houston Museum District",
CITE, Houston, Spring, pp. 8-15
-Stein, Karen D., "Texas Two-Step", ARCHITECTURAL RECORD,
Record Houses 1996, New York, April, pp. 90-93
-Ingersoll, Richard, "Carlos Jimenez", Monograph, A + U, No. 306,
Tokyo, March
-Riera Ojeda, Oscar, Editor, "Carlos Jimenez", Monograph, CASAS
INTERNATIONAL, No. 41, Kliczkowski Publishers, Buenos Aires
-Ghirardo, Diane, "ARCHITECTURE AFTER MODERNISM",
Thames and Hudson, London
-Adria, Miquel, "Arquitecturas Ancladas, Carlos Jimenez", ARQUITEC-
TURA, Mexico City, January-February, pp. 4-5, 36-47
**1995**
-Tzonis, A./ Lefaivre, L./ Diamond, R., "ARCHITECTURE IN
NORTH AMERICA SINCE 1960", Little, Brown and Co., New York,
London, pp. 53-54, 242-245
-"581 ARCHITECTS IN THE WORLD", Gallery Ma, Toto, Tokyo,
p. 361
-"FIFTY FROM FIFTY", The Atrium Press, College of Architecture,
University of Houston
-Russell, Beverly, "40 UNDER 40", Vitae Publishers, Grand Rapids,
pp. 166-173.
-Riera Ojeda, Oscar, Editor, "THE NEW AMERICAN HOUSE",
The Whitney Library of Design, New York, pp. 102-105
-Zabalbeascoa, Anatxu, "THE HOUSE OF THE ARCHITECT",
Editorial Gustavo Gili/Rizzoli, Barcelona, New York, pp. 90-95
-Cifra, Juliana, "Carlos Jimenez, Un Poeta de la Arquitectura", AXXIS,
No. 38, Medellin, November, pp. 10-16
-Hagen Hodgson, Petra, "Carlos Jimenez: Suche nach bleibenden
Werten", BAUDOC BULLETIN, Basel, November, pp. 1-2, 5-14

-Withers, Jane, "Homework", INDEPENDENT MAGAZINE, London, November 4, p. 28

-Barna, Joel Warren, "Glendower Court and Melanie Court", CITE, Houston, Fall, p. 25

-Russell, Beverly, "Forty Under Forty", INTERIORS, New York, September, p. 72

-Zabalbeascoa, Anatxu, "Mis edificios buscan estimular la vida interior, Entrevista", EL PAIS, Babelia, Madrid, June 10, p. 17

-Moix, Llatzer, "Cuando el arquitecto es su propio cliente", LA VAN-GUARDIA, Cultura, Barcelona, June 4, p. 60

-Burchard, Peter, "For Art's Sake: The Spencer Studio Art Building", WILLIAMS ALUMNI REVIEW, Williamstown, Spring, pp. 18-23

-Doroshenko, Peter, Ed., "Carlos Jimenez on the Urban Situation", ARTLIES, Houston, April-May, pp. 26-27

- "Addition to Houston Museum Campus", PROGRESSIVE ARCHI-TECTURE, Stamford, March, p. 23

-Moorhead, Gerald, "Arts Campus", ARCHITECTURAL RECORD, New York, January, pp. 70-79

**1994**

-Velasco Facio, Hector, "INTERVENTED SPACES", Catalogue to the Exhibition, Museo de Arte Carrillo Gil, Mexico City, pp. 8-11

-Guell, Xavier, "CATALOGOS DE ARQUITECTURA CONTEMPO-RANEA", Editorial Gustavo Gili, Barcelona, pp. 96-103

-Webb, Michael, "ARCHITECTS HOUSE THEMSELVES", The Preservation Press, Washington D.C., pp. 95-97

-"BEST LAID PLANS", Rice Design Alliance, Catalogue to the Exhibition, Houston, p. 31

-Croset, Pierre-Alain, "Edifici Urbani a Houston di Jimenez", CASABELLA, No. 615, Milan, September, pp. 6-15, 68-69

-"Pieza de Resistencia", ARQUITECTURA VIVA, No. 38, Madrid, September/October, pp. 54-61, 119

-Quintana, Claudia Veronica, "Blanco y Negro", CASAS & GENTE, Mexico City, October, pp. 74-76

-Loomis, John, "Other Americas", DESIGN BOOK REVIEW, Berkeley, Summer, pp. 2, 101

-Reynoso Pohlenz, Jorge, "Museo de Bellas Artes de Houston", ENLACE, Mexico City, August, pp. 52-55

-Burchard, Linda, "Vision of New Art Center at Williams College", THE BERKSHIRE EAGLE, Pittsfield, May 3, p. B5

-Moorhead, Gerald, "Urbane Modesty", ARCHITECTURAL RECORD, Record Houses 1994, New York, April, pp. 96-99

-Riera Ojeda, Oscar, Editor, "Viviendas en Estados Unidos", CASAS INTERNACIONAL, No. 30, Kliczkowski Publishers, Buenos Aires, pp. 8-13

-Chadwick, Susan, "New Building opens up M.F.A.", HOUSTON POST, March 19, p. F1

-Holmes, Ann, "M.F.A. expansion is elegant visually as well as thematically", HOUSTON CHRONICLE, March 17, pp. C1, C5

-"Carlos Jimenez en el Williams College", ARQUITECTURA VIVA, No. 34, Madrid, January-February, p. 11

**1993**

-Bullivant, Lucy, "INTERNATIONAL INTERIORS 4", Thames and Hudson, London, pp. 218-219

-"Recent Six Works by Carlos Jimenez", A + U, No. 279, Tokyo,

December, pp. 64-99

-Ghirardo, Diane, "Carlos Jimenez, Prove di Stabilita", LOTUS INTERNATIONAL, No. 77, Milan, Summer, pp. 1, 46-57

-"Fabrica Ligera, Casa Chadwick, Houston", ARQUITECTURA VIVA, No. 31, Madrid, July-August, pp. 1, 46-49

-Fox, Stephen, "Administration and Junior School Building Museum of Fine Arts, CITE, Houston, Spring-Summer, p. 3

-Cadell, Erin, "Jimenez ponders artistic mission", THE WILLIAMS RECORD, Williamstown, April 20, p. 1

-Holmes, Ann, "Lean Poetry of Carlos Jimenez", HOUSTON CHRONICLE, Zest Magazine, April 4, pp. 2, 12-13, 18

-_____, "Artful Structure", HOUSTON CHRONICLE, March 31, pp. 1D, 6D

-Sainz, Jorge, "Una Cabana entre Robles", A & V, No. 39, Madrid, pp. 93-103

**1992**

-Dillon, David, "Jimenez on Jimenez", ELLE DECOR, New York, October/November, pp. 136-143

-"Nos visito Carlos Jimenez", LA NACION-VIVIENDA, San Jose, October 8, p. 4C

-Wamble, Mark, "Five Houses: Domesticity and the Contingent City", CITE, Houston, Fall, pp. 64-67

-"Sketchbooks: What comes out of them", ARCHITECTURE OF ISRAEL, No. 13, Tel-Aviv, August, pp. 64-67

-Moorhead, Gerald, "For Art's Sake", ARCHITECTURAL RECORD, New York, August, pp. 77, 84-89

-Jarmusch, Ann, "Architects told to see the light", THE SAN DIEGO UNION TRIBUNE, July 5, p. F12

-Norten, Enrique, "Luz, Color, Espacio, La arquitectura de Carlos Jimenez", ARQUITECTURA, Mexico City, Spring, pp. 54-57

-Green, Mary, "The Architect's Sketchbook - Ten Contemporary Architects", HABITEC, Montreal, March 20

-Resse, Carol McMichael, "THE ARCHITECT'S SKETCHBOOK: CURRENT PRACTICE", Catalogue to the Exhibition, Canadian Center for Architecture, Montreal, p. 6, pp. 18-19

-Moiraghi, Luigi, "La nuova fusione americana: Carlos Jimenez Latin American architecture", L'ARCA, No. 57, Milan, March, p. 105

-Reese, Carol McMichael, "Retiro de Coleccionista", ARQUITECTURA VIVA, No. 23, Madrid, March-April, pp. 3, 40-43

-Rasch, Horst, "Hier Begann Architekt Als Archaologe", HAUSER, Hamburg, January, p. 22-27

**1991**

-Rossi, Aldo; Forster, Kurt W., "CARLOS JIMENEZ", Monograph, Editorial Gustavo Gili, Barcelona

-Parks, Janet, "CONTEMPORARY ARCHITECTURAL DRAW-INGS", Avery Library Centennial Drawings Archive, Pomegranate Press, San Francisco

-Amourgis, Spyros, "CRITICAL REGIONALISM", California State Polytechnic University Books, Pomona, pp. 61-68

-Bullivant, Lucy, "INTERNATIONAL INTERIORS 3", Thames and Hudson, London, pp. 58-59

-Lacy, Bill, "100 CONTEMPORARY ARCHITECTS AND THEIR DRAWINGS", Harry N. Abrams, New York, pp. 120-121

-Dillon, David, "Shaping the Spaces of Texas", SOUTHERN

ACCENTS, Birmingham, December, pp. 46-52

-Faerna, Jose Maria, "Libros: Carlos Jimenez", DISENO INTERIOR, Madrid, December, p. 86

-Fernandez Galiano, Luis, "Carlos Blue", ARQUITECTURA VIVA, No. 21, Madrid, November-December, p. 61

-"Books: Carlos Jimenez", INTERIOR DESIGN, New York, November, p. 72

-Moore, Barry, "Goode becomes Great", HOUSTON PRESS, November 14-20, p. 18

-Grane, Jorge, "La arquitectura de Carlos Jimenez", LA NACION, San Jose, November 14, p. 2

-Lavin, Sylvia, "Filling in the Blank, Carlos Jimenez", A + U, No. 251, Tokyo, August, pp. 80-116

-Holmes, Ann, "Museum of Fine Arts Exhibition Pavillion planned", HOUSTON CHRONICLE, February 23

-Chadwick, Susan, "M.F.A. selects Houston architect to design new Montrose building", HOUSTON POST, February 20

**1990**

-Brauer, Deborah, "PROJECT HOUSTON", Catalogue to the Exhibition, Diverse Works Gallery, Houston, pp. 40-41

-Fox, Stephen, "HOUSTON ARCHITECTURAL GUIDE", American Institute of Architects, Houston Chapter

-"U.S.A./U.S.S.R. 1980-1990, The Socially Responsible Environment", A.D.P.S.R., Catalogue to the Exhibition, New York-Moscow

-"Carlos Jimenez en Houston", LA NACION-VIVIENDA 1, San Jose, November, p. 8C

-"House along the Bayou", NIKKEI ARCHITECTURE, Tokyo, October, pp. 195198

-"Carlos Jimenez conversa con Aldo Rossi", HABITAR, No. 31, San Jose, September, pp. 32-33

-Dibar, L. Carlos, "Las Casas de Carlos Jimenez", ARQUITECTURA Y CONSTRUCCION, Buenos Aires, July 11, pp. 7-8

-Radice, Barbara; Marquez, Viola, "Carlos Jimenez", TERRAZZO, No. 4, Milan, Spring, pp. 19, 109-116

-"Four Projects", QUADERNS D'ARQUITECTURA I URBANISME, No. 184, Barcelona, January-March, pp. 64-65

-Anderson, Grace, "Blue Bayou", ARCHITECTURAL RECORD, Record Houses 1990, New York, April, pp. 48-51

-Dillon, David, "Light Geometry", HOUSE & GARDEN, New York, March, pp. 168-173

-McKay, Gary, "A Personal Angle", HOUSTON METROPOLITAN, February, pp. 5457

-Sartain, Sophie, "Carlos Jimenez", HOUSTON POST, January 14, pp. F1, F6

**1989**

-Ingersoll, Richard, "El Espiritu de los Silos, Carlos Jimenez en Houston", ARQUITECTURA VIVA, No. 8, Madrid, October, pp. 28-31

-Barriere, Philippe, "Maison d'edition a Houston", L'ARCHITECTURE D'AUJOURD'HUI, No. 263, Paris, June, pp. 112-113

-"Young American Designers: Carlos Jimenez", DESIGN U.S.A., United States Information Agency, Summer, Washington, p. 61

-Rieselbach, Anne, "Carlos Jimenez", ELLE, New York, June, p. 42

-Barna, Joel Warren, "Texas Houses: Context vs. Subtext", TEXAS ARCHITECT, Austin, May-June, pp. 1, 29, 31

-Anderton, Frances, "Cool Work by Jimenez", THE ARCHITECTURAL REVIEW, London, March, pp. 27, 64-69

**1988**

-"La visita de un arquitecto costarricense: Carlos Jimenez", HABITAR, No. 27, San Jose, December, pp. 23-24, 44, 47-48

-"New Works by Carlos Jimenez", DOMAIN, Austin, Fall, p. 29

-Bartle, Andrew, "The Big Country: Young American architects west of the Mississippi", OTTAGONO, No. 90, Milan, September-November, p. 29

**1987**

-Zevon, Susan, "Three Roofs over his Head", HOUSE BEAUTIFUL, New York, November, pp. 104-109, 111

-"Carlos Jimenez Estudio de Arquitectura", HABITAR, No. 23, San Jose, July, p. 27

-Fisher, Thomas, "Young Architects: Carlos Jimenez", PROGRESSIVE ARCHITECTURE, Stamford, June, pp. 92-93

-Hartman, William, "Work of Emerging Architects", CITE, Spring, Houston, p. 19

**1986**

-Hahn, Wilhelm, "Houston Fine Art Press Building", CITE, Spring, Houston, p. 21

-"De Regreso a lo Basico", HABITAR, No. 19, San Jose, March, p. 16

-Schmertz, Mildred, "True Privacy", ARCHITECTURAL RECORD, New York, March, pp. 124-127

**1985**

-Roberts, Raquel, "Back to Basics", HOUSTON HOME & GARDEN, September, pp. 28-31

-Fuller, Larry Paul, "Solo Abode", TEXAS HOMES, Austin, September, pp. 7273, 112-114

# PROJECTS CREDIT

**JIMENEZ HOUSE AND STUDIO**
(1983-1993)
Carlos Jimenez, Designer
Dominique Brousseau, Robert Fowler

**HOUSTON FINE ART PRESS**
(1985-1987)
Carlos Jimenez, Designer

**LYNN GOODE GALLERY**
(1990-1991)
Carlos Jimenez, Designer
Dominique Brousseau

**DRIVE-IN LIBRARY**
(1990)
Carlos Jimenez, Designer
Domminique Brousseau

**CENTRAL ADMINISTRATION AND JUNIOR SCHOOL
BUILDING, MUSEUM OF FINE ARTS, HOUSTON**
(1991-1994)
CARLOS JIMENEZ ARCHITECTURE STUDIO, Design Architect
Carlos Jimenez, Designer, John H. Bowley, project architect,
Dominique Brousseau, Robert Fowler, Eric Batte, David Lee, Mason
Wickham
KENDALL/HEATON ASSOCIATES, INC., Associate Architects
Bill Kendall, Lary Burns, project architect, Warren Carpenter

**ART LEAGUE OF HOUSTON**
(1994-1996)
Carlos Jimenez, Designer
Robert Fowler, John H. Bowley, Eric Batte, Chad Johnson

**IRWIN UNION BANK BRANCH PROTOTYPE**
(1995-1996)
CARLOS JIMENEZ ARCHITECTURE STUDIO, Design Architect
Carlos Jimenez, Designer
Robert Fowler, Chad Johnson
TODD WILLIAMS ARCHITECT, Associate Architect

**SPENCER STUDIO ART BUILDING, WILLIAMS COLLEGE**
(1993- 1996)
CARLOS JIMENEZ ARCHITECTURE STUDIO, Design Architect
Carlos Jimenez, Designer, John H. Bowley, project architect;
Robert Fowler, Eric Batte, Mason Wickham, Joaquin Diz
CAMBRIDGE SEVEN ASSOCIATES, INC., Associate Architects
Dick Tuve, Bob Galloway, project architects; Melissa Douglas